ASHE Higher Education Report: Volume 36, Number 6
Kelly Ward, Lisa E. Wolf-Wendel, Series Editors

Racial and Ethnic Minority Students' Success in STEM Education

Samuel D. Museus

Robert T. Palmer

Ryan J. Davis

Dina C. Maramba

Racial and Ethnic Minority Students' Success in STEM Education
Samuel D. Museus, Robert T. Palmer, Ryan J. Davis, and Dina C. Maramba
ASHE Higher Education Report: Volume 36, Number 6
Kelly Ward, Lisa E. Wolf-Wendel, Series Editors

ISSN 1551-6970   electronic ISSN 1554-6306   ISBN 978-1-1180-6586-0

The ASHE Higher Education Report is part of the Jossey-Bass Higher and Adult
Education Series and is published six times a year by Wiley Subscription Services,
Inc., A Wiley Company, at Jossey-Bass, 989 Market Street, San Francisco,
California 94103-1741.

For subscription information, see the Back Issue/Subscription Order Form
in the back of this volume.

CALL FOR PROPOSALS: Prospective authors are strongly encouraged to contact
Kelly Ward (kaward@wsu.edu) or Lisa Wolf-Wendel (lwolf@ku.edu). See "About
the ASHE Higher Education Report Series" in the back of this volume.

Visit the Jossey-Bass Web site at **www.josseybass.com.**

Printed in the United States of America on acid-free recycled paper.

The ASHE Higher Education Report is indexed in CIJE: Current Index to Jour-
nals in Education (ERIC), Current Abstracts (EBSCO), Education Index/Abstracts
(H.W. Wilson), ERIC Database (Education Resources Information Center),
Higher Education Abstracts (Claremont Graduate University), IBR & IBZ: Inter-
national Bibliographies of Periodical Literature (K.G. Saur), and Resources in
Education (ERIC).

Advisory Board

ASHE

The ASHE Higher Education Report Series is sponsored by the Association for the Study of Higher Education (ASHE), which provides an editorial advisory board of ASHE members.

Contents

Executive Summary

Increasing the success of racial and ethnic minority students in science, technology, engineering, and mathematics (STEM) has become a critical issue. Indeed, several trends underscore the importance of fostering success among minority students in STEM education. For example, according to U.S. Census Bureau projections, racial and ethnic minorities are expected to account for more than half the national population by 2050. This demographic shift means that minority students will make up an increasingly larger percentage of students in the national education system and STEM talent pool. Yet relatively low rates of success among minority students in STEM education persist. Thus, understanding how to maximize success among racial and ethnic minorities in STEM education is evermore critical.

Existing evidence indicates that several factors may significantly influence the success of racial and ethnic minority students in STEM. In K–12, scholars have underscored the critical link between underpreparedness and a lack of success in STEM education. Several K–12 factors appear to be responsible for the underpreparedness of minorities in STEM:

- Disparities in the funding of public schools, which leave schools that serve large numbers of minority students underresourced;
- An overrepresentation of unqualified teachers in schools that serve high numbers of minority students;
- Limited opportunities to take Advanced Placement courses;
- Systems that disproportionately track minority students into remedial courses;

- Teachers' low expectations of racial and ethnic minority students;
- Stereotype threats that undermine minority students' academic performance;
- Racial oppression and oppositional culture; and
- Premature departure from high school.

Several K–12 factors, however, positively influence the success of racial and ethnic minority students in STEM, including:

- Parental involvement and support;
- The availability of bilingual education;
- Culturally relevant pedagogy;
- Early exposure to STEM fields;
- Interest in STEM careers;
- Self-efficacy in STEM subjects; and
- STEM opportunity and support programs.

In higher education, researchers have uncovered several factors that can influence the success of racial and ethnic minority students in STEM majors, including:

- Colorblind meritocracy and affirmative action;
- Economic factors such as financial aid and employment experiences;
- Institutional type;
- Campus culture and climate;
- Institutional agents;
- Psychological factors such as self-concept and self-efficacy; and
- STEM opportunity and support programs.

The comprehensive review, analysis, and synthesis of this literature reveal several important implications for educational research, policy, and practice. Educational researchers, for example, should consider:

- The need to understand racial and ethnic minority groups in more complex ways through disaggregated analyses;
- The importance of developing a greater understanding of parental influences on minority students' success in STEM;

- The need to fill gaps in knowledge about how attending specific types of institutions influences success in STEM;
- The importance of understanding the experiences of minority students in STEM at community colleges; and
- The gap in research that employs rigorous methods to understand whether STEM-specific opportunity and support programs are effective and inquiries that illuminate how they facilitate success among minority students.

In light of existing evidence, education policymakers should consider:

- The importance of ensuring that minority students are not incorrectly tracked into remedial coursework and have access to Advanced Placement courses;
- Attracting highly qualified teachers to schools with large numbers of racial and ethnic minorities through the use of incentives;
- The importance of offering sufficient numbers of Advanced Placement courses;
- Policies to achieve equity in the distribution of resources across school districts;
- The value of supporting bilingual education; and
- Cultural and socioeconomic contexts in policy efforts, including the importance of cultural community engagement and ensuring sufficient need-based aid for low-income students in college.

Finally, the literature on minority students in STEM education suggests that K–12 and postsecondary educators should give attention to several considerations:

- Seeking funding to create, expand, or build on the outreach programs that have demonstrated effectiveness;
- Emphasizing peer collaboration and community as well as research experiences in STEM;
- Creating classroom cultures with collectivist values that emphasize the success of all students and send a message to those students that they can succeed in STEM;

- Making conscious efforts to connect STEM curricula to current events and minority students' communities; and
- Exposing minority students to opportunities and careers in STEM early and throughout their STEM education.

Much remains to be learned about racial and ethnic minority students in STEM education. Nevertheless, by understanding the evidence that does exist and considering the implications of that evidence, educational researchers, policymakers, and practitioners can maximize their ability to foster success among the minority students whom they serve.

Foreword

Recently some colleagues and I at the University of Kansas were looking at some K–12 transcript data that had been linked to the National Student Clearinghouse. In analyzing that data, we concluded that the most important factor in predicting whether high school students go to college, go to a four-year college, attend a selective college, and make timely progress toward graduating from college is their high school math performance (highest level of math taken and grade point average in math courses). All other predictors paled in comparison. Our findings mirror those of other scholars, including Adelman (1999) and Drew (1996), who concluded that math education in K–12 is important to future success. We have known this for quite a while, yet the solution of getting a wider array of students to partake in advanced math classes and perform well in math has eluded us. Indeed we live in a society in which it is normal for people to proudly proclaim, "I don't do math," almost wearing it as a badge of honor. In contrast, we tend to discourage people from saying "I don't do writing" or "I don't do reading," as we recognize that these statements flout ignorance. The problem is that math is the gateway to future academic success: the gateway to college, to the most lucrative careers, and to solving some of the most important social concerns of our day—global warming, safe energy, and space exploration, to name a few. Achievement in mathematics is also the gateway to achievement in science, engineering, and technology.

The United States has performed poorly in math and science compared with other countries, which has caused a fair amount of concern among policymakers and the public. Math woes in the United States are exacerbated by the fact that not everyone has equal access to or success in mathematics. In particular, the fact that racial and ethnic minority students often attend K–12 schools that are inadequately prepared to teach upper-level math classes and are discouraged from pursuing advanced math leads to the problem of not having enough highly qualified students pursuing postsecondary degrees in science, technology, engineering, and mathematics (STEM).

Not having young people from diverse racial and ethnic backgrounds pursuing math and science interests in K–12 leads to problems with the STEM pipeline at all levels. Without adequate preparation, students are less likely to pursue undergraduate majors in STEM, less likely to pursue graduate degrees, and therefore less likely to serve as faculty members at colleges and universities in these fields. It also makes racial and ethnic minorities less likely to pursue other scientific careers and to further the research agenda in STEM. The lack of diversity at all levels creates a self-reinforcing cycle where the lack of role models at every level leads to fewer individuals at all levels. It is important to note that the lack of diversity in STEM is not about a lack of individual interest or aptitude: it is a systemic problem starting in the K–12 system and continuing at the undergraduate, graduate, and professional levels. These systemic concerns are the focus of this monograph on racial and ethnic minorities in STEM.

This monograph by Sam Museus, Robert Palmer, Ryan Davis, and Dina Maramba focuses a thoughtful lens on the systemic problems leading to underrepresentation of racial and ethnic minorities in STEM fields. It focuses on the K–12 system as well as on the systemic concerns in higher education. One unique facet of this particular monograph is that it includes an in-depth discussion of Asian American and Pacific Islander and Native American students. The inclusion of these two groups in the monograph is important because they are often left out of discussions of minorities in STEM (and higher education in general), which tend to focus on Black and Latina and Latino issues. In addition, one noteworthy element of this monograph is that it focuses on models of success and on findings factors that can positively change the systems. All too often, the focus is on explaining failure. It is refreshing to read about instances and processes that have yielded positive outcomes. This positive slant does not underestimate the problems, however; it provides hope that solutions can be found. The model in the final chapter represents an important visual summation of the literature reviewed and will serve as a useful framework for researchers who study minorities in STEM in the future.

This monograph should be read in conjunction with other ASHE monographs on related topics, including Daryl Smith's monograph on the diversity challenge (2005), Watson Scott Swail's monograph on retaining minority students (2003), and Marybeth Walpole's monograph on economically and educationally challenged students (2007). It is an important read for educational researchers, faculty, and graduate students who seek the latest research about racial and ethnic minority students in STEM. It is also an important piece for practitioners and policymakers who are actively working to improve the science and mathematics pipeline for historically underrepresented minority students. This monograph brings a welcome perspective and expertise to an important problem facing education and society at large. We are proud to include it as part of the ASHE Higher Education Report series.

Lisa E. Wolf-Wendel
Series Editor

Acknowledgments

The authors would like to thank several people. Samuel D. Museus is indebted to his colleagues at the University of Massachusetts Boston, who have provided intellectual and professional support throughout the production of this monograph. He would especially like to thank Hannah Sevian and Carol L. Colbeck for their collaborative work in STEM education, which informed the production of this monograph. He would also like to thank his graduate research assistants, Deborah Liverman and Joanna N. Ravello, who provided support for the production of this volume. Robert T. Palmer would like to thank James Moore III for helping to cultivate his interest in STEM education. Ryan J. Davis wishes to acknowledge the faculty and participants involved in the 2009 ASHE Institute on Critical Research and Policy Analysis for their contributions to his thinking about equity issues in higher education. Dina C. Maramba wishes to thank the Department of Student Affairs administration at the State University of New York, Binghamton. All four authors are thankful for one another's contributions to the positive collaborative experience throughout the composition of this volume.

Dedications

Samuel D. Museus dedicates this monograph to his brother, Andrew Museus, who has devoted his life to providing opportunities and support for disadvantaged youth in K–12 schools. Robert T. Palmer wishes to dedicate this work to the late Dr. Vernon C. Polite, who exemplified "manly deeds, scholarship, and love for all mankind." Ryan J. Davis dedicates this work to Christina Annette Jones for her spiritual uplift and pastoral care during the period of time he contributed to this monograph. Dina C. Maramba would like to dedicate this monograph to her family and friends. Their unwavering love and support continue to inspire her work.

Published online in Wiley Online Library
(wileyonlinelibrary.com) • DOI: 10.1002/aehe.3606

Introduction, Context, and Overview of the Volume

> To neglect the science education of any is to deprive them of basic education, handicap them for life, and deprive the nation of talented workers and informed citizens—a loss the nation can ill afford.
>
> —American Association for the Advancement of Science, 1989, p. 214

FOSTERING SUCCESS among racial and ethnic minority[1] students in science, technology, engineering, and mathematics (STEM) has never been more important to our nation. The Business–Higher Education Forum (2005) underscored this point when it asserted that "increased global competition, lackluster performance in mathematics and science education, and a lack of national focus on renewing its science and technology infrastructure have created a new economic and technological vulnerability as serious as any military or terrorist threat" (p. 3). As we discuss in the following sections, at a time when our nation is becoming more racially and ethnically diverse, the economy is increasingly global, and racial and ethnic disparities persist, educators must better understand how to increase the number of minority students entering higher education in the pursuit of STEM degrees, graduating from college in STEM majors, and joining the STEM workforce with adequate preparation.

The National Context: Important Trends in Racial Demographics and STEM Fields

Two major trends provide important context for our discussion of racial and ethnic minority students' success in the STEM circuit.[2] First, the racial and ethnic diversity of the nation, and therefore diversity of the STEM talent pool, is increasing rapidly. Second, existing evidence indicates that high rates of departure, particularly among minority students, from the STEM education circuit persist. This section provides an overview of these trends.

National demographic data convey one reality very clearly: America is becoming more diverse at an unprecedented rate. In fact, recent U.S. Census Bureau (2008) projections indicate that racial and ethnic minorities will make up more than half the national population by 2050. Some groups will grow more rapidly than others (see Figure 1). For example, Asian American and Pacific Islanders (AAPIs) and Hispanics currently constitute 5 percent and 16 percent of the national population, respectively, but are projected to account for about 8 percent and 30 percent of the population by 2050. Meanwhile, according to those same estimates, Blacks and Native Americans will grow at much slower paces and continue to account for approximately 13 percent and 1 percent, respectively, of the population in 2050. On the other hand, the proportion of the national population that is of European descent will decline over the next four decades. As a result of these shifting demographics, racial and ethnic minorities will make up a growing proportion of students making their way through the education system and the supply of potential future STEM students and professionals. These shifts also mean that the growing numbers of minority students will make up a larger proportion of America's resources; moreover, they are assets that educators must tap to effectively use the talent available in America's diverse student bodies.

Another trend that provides important context for this volume is the high rates of departure from and failure in STEM education. Many realities contribute to this problem: many students' lack of interest in STEM fields, inadequate preparation among high school graduates for STEM majors, and students who leave STEM majors or drop out all together. For example, the percentage of ACT college entrance test takers interested in majoring in engineering or computer and

Figure 1
Census Bureau Population Projections, by Race, from 2010 to 2050

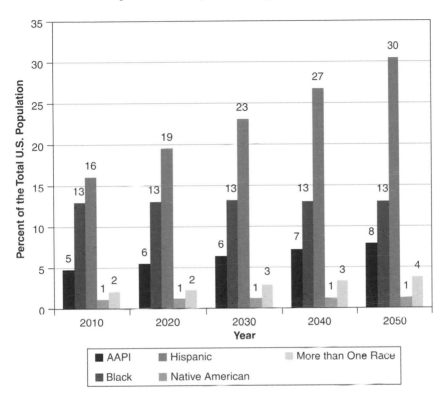

Source: U.S. Census Bureau, 2008.

information science is declining (ACT, Inc., 2006). Moreover, of high school graduates who take the ACT examination, fewer than half exceed college readiness benchmarks for math (41 percent) and science (26 percent). Although ACT has not reported these numbers for specific racial groups, racial and ethnic minority students are even less adequately prepared than their White counterparts. As many as 65 percent of college students who enter STEM majors do not complete a degree within six years of matriculation (National Center for Education Statistics, 2009). Moreover, the numbers are even worse for many groups of color, with less than 16 percent of Black, Hispanic, and Native American college students who aspire to earn a bachelor's degree in STEM actually accomplishing that goal within five years of matriculation (Higher Education Research Institute, 2010).

Multiple trends provide important context for researching, understanding, and improving racial and ethnic minority students' success in STEM. Increasing diversification of the potential STEM student body and workforce and high rates of departure from the STEM education circuit suggest that we urgently need to better understand how to foster success among all students in general and minority students in STEM in particular. The following section discusses the current condition of racial and ethnic minorities in STEM education.

The Urgency of Fostering Minority Students' Success in STEM

Increasing the success of racial and ethnic minority students in the STEM circuit is essential for several reasons, both financial and social. First, increasing success among those students has important implications for their financial well-being (Baum and Payea, 2005; Carnevale and Desrochers, 2003; Choy and Li, 2005; Kelly, 2005). For example, the annual individual income of high school graduates on average is approximately 62 percent that of four-year college graduates (Baum and Payea, 2005). Thus, increasing the success of racial and ethnic minorities in the STEM circuit translates into greater individual rewards and economic returns (Palmer, Davis, Moore, and Hilton, 2010). These considerations should be of paramount importance to educational researchers, policymakers, and practitioners.

Second, increased success among racial and ethnic minority students in STEM is associated with maintaining America's competitiveness in the global marketplace. In fact, several high-profile organizations have warned that the nation's standing in the global economy is declining and the preparation of graduates who can contribute to its scientific and technological capacity is critical to preventing further decline and maintaining the nation's competitiveness in the international marketplace (American Council on Education, 2006; Committee on Prospering in the Global Economy of the 21st Century, 2007; National Action Council for Minorities in Engineering, 2008). The Committee on Prospering in the Global Economy of the 21st Century, for example, stated, "Having reviewed trends in the

United States and abroad, the committee is deeply concerned that the scientific and technological building blocks critical to our economic leadership are eroding at a time when many other nations are gathering strength" (p. 3). In doing so, the committee highlighted the urgency of producing graduates who can effectively contribute to the STEM workforce and vibrancy of our economy. Given our earlier assertions that minorities will make up an increasingly larger proportion of the STEM talent pool, it is essential for educators to maximize the success of these individuals if they are to use the entire talent pool of potential STEM college students, college graduates, and professionals who can help maintain America's edge in the global marketplace.

In addition to these individual and national economic concerns, and perhaps more important, maximizing the success of racial and ethnic minorities in the STEM education circuit is a moral and ethical imperative. As we illustrate later in this chapter, by virtually every indicator and at every level of education, racial and ethnic minority students suffer from persisting systemic inequities in the STEM circuit. Later in the volume, we discuss economic (such as disparities in funding), cultural (the Eurocentric curricula), racial (prejudice and discrimination), and structural factors that contribute to the systemic limiting of opportunities among racial and ethnic minority students. We argue that it is the moral and ethical obligation of all educators to work against such unfair systemic forms of inequality.

Finally, it is also critical for our education system to foster success among racial and ethnic minority students in the STEM circuit because greater racial and ethnic diversity in STEM fields contributes to the enhanced ability of all members of the STEM workforce to function effectively in an increasingly diverse and global economy. Indeed, both empirical evidence and industry leaders' perspectives suggest that a more diverse student body in STEM fields leads to a workforce of scientists, engineers, and mathematicians who are more equipped to function effectively in today's diverse and global workforce (see, for example, Chang, 2007; Denson and Chang, 2009) and contribute productively to new scientific, technological, and medical discoveries to maintain America's status as a leader in the global marketplace.

In sum, increasing success among racial and ethnic minority students in STEM is urgent for several reasons, including the fact that it is necessary for the economic well-being of individuals and the nation, America's competitiveness in the international marketplace, the moral and ethical obligation of educators to fight systemic inequities, and the need to adequately prepare STEM college graduates for the increasingly diverse and global STEM workforce.

Purpose and Overview of the Volume

The primary purpose of this monograph is to provide educational researchers, policymakers, and practitioners with an overview of existing knowledge regarding factors that influence success among racial and ethnic minority students in the STEM circuit. To accomplish this task, we reviewed more than four hundred books, book chapters, journal articles, and policy reports related to this topic. The remainder of this opening chapter discusses the current condition of racial and ethnic minorities in STEM education, paying particular attention to racial disparities throughout the circuit. It also discusses the role of race in the experiences of racial and ethnic minorities in STEM. The following two chapters provide a comprehensive synthesis and analysis of the literature on the precollege and college-level factors that influence the success of students of color in the STEM circuit. The final chapter presents the Racial and Ethnic Minorities in STEM (REM STEM) model, which emerged from our review of the literature, to serve as a framework to guide future research, policy, and practice. This concluding chapter also offers implications for future research, policy, and practice.

Key Concepts and Definitions

Before we begin our analysis and synthesis of existing literature on racial and ethnic minority students in STEM education, it is critical to define key concepts and note important limitations of the volume. This section delineates and defines terms related to race, ethnicity, and STEM education. In defining these concepts, we aim to establish clarity and consistency in our word choices and the meanings that we attach to them. Building on extant literature (for example, Helms, 1994; Museus and Kiang, 2009; Torres, Howard-Hamilton, and Cooper, 2003; U.S. Census Bureau, 2004a, 2004b, 2004c, 2004d, 2004e;

Yinger, 1994), we use the following definitions for key race-related terms in this volume:

Race: We use this term to refer to categorizations that are created by humankind based on the hereditary traits of different groups of people, thereby creating socially constructed distinctions. We recognize that racial identification is complicated and that racial categories overlap, meaning that one person can fit into two or more of the racial categories delineated below.

Ethnicity: This word refers to an identity based on a person's nationality or tribal group. Each racial group consists of many different ethnicities. For the purposes of this volume, ethnicity is an identity based on membership in a segment of a larger society that does not share the same culture with other segments of society.

Racial and ethnic minority students: We use this term to refer to students who identify as Asian American and Pacific Islander (AAPI), Black, Hispanic, or Native American. Although we would typically include mixed-race individuals in this definition, we exclude them from our definition and discussion in this volume because most—in fact, almost all—of the existing research on minority students in STEM fails to pay specific attention to this population, which we recognize as a major limitation of existing knowledge, research, and discourse around racial and ethnic minorities in the STEM circuit.

Asian American and Pacific Islander: Although Asian Americans and Pacific Islanders are two distinct groups, they are often lumped together under this term and categorized as one race. Where we discuss statistics or literature that refers to both groups, we use the term "Asian American and Pacific Islander," which refers to a person with origins in East Asia, Southeast Asia, the Indian subcontinent, or the Pacific Islands. *Asian Americans* include, but are not limited to, Americans of Bangladeshi, Cambodian, Chinese, Filipino, Hmong, (Asian) Indian, Indonesian, Japanese, Korean, Laotian, Malaysian, Pakistani, Sri Lankan, Taiwanese, Thai, and Vietnamese descent. *Pacific Islanders* include, but are not limited to, Native Hawaiian, Guamanian/Chamorro, Samoan, Tongan, and Fijian groups.

Black: We use this word to refer to persons with origins in any of the Black racial groups of Africa or persons with ethnic origins in the Black racial groups of the Caribbean, Central America, South America, and other regions of the world.

Hispanic: We use this term to refer to persons having ethnic origins in the peoples of Mexico, Puerto Rico, Cuba, Central America, South America, or other Spanish cultures and communities. This word includes groups who identify as Chicano, Latino, and Mexican American.

Native American: This word refers to a person having ethnic origins in the indigenous peoples of North America and who identifies with indigenous tribes or communities. This category includes American Indians and Native Alaskans.

White: We use this term to refer to persons with ethnic origins in the peoples of Europe, White peoples of North Africa, or peoples of the Middle East.

In addition, borrowing and building on terminology from the National Science Foundation (NSF, 2010a), we designate and define the following STEM-related terms:

Science fields: These fields include environmental (earth sciences, oceanography), life (agricultural, biological, medical sciences), and physical (astronomy, chemistry, physics) sciences.

Technology fields: These fields include computer sciences (computer and information science as well as management information systems).

Engineering fields: These fields include aeronautical, astronautical, bioengineering and biomedical, chemical, civil, electrical, and mechanical engineering.

Mathematics fields: These fields include general mathematics, applied mathematics, and mathematical statistics.

STEM circuit: We choose not to use the common term "STEM pipeline," because scholars have deemed this term an inadequate label for the multiple and varying pathways that students take though the STEM system (Adelman, 2006). Rather, we employ the term "STEM circuit" in this volume. We define the

STEM circuit as a system of the multiple and varying educational pathways from science and math education in elementary school to completion of terminal STEM degrees (such as the Ph.D.). Our analysis and synthesis of literature focus on the pathways in the circuit from elementary education to the completion of a bachelor's degree.

Success in the STEM circuit: For the purpose of this volume, our definition of "success in the STEM circuit" is multifaceted. It encompasses the adequate preparation of students in math and science before entering college as well as the adequate academic performance, persistence, and completion of baccalaureate degrees in science, technology, engineering, and mathematics majors. It should be noted, however, that we do recognize that other equally valid definitions exist of success in the STEM circuit that might include constructs such as satisfaction in STEM majors, development of STEM-related knowledge, completion of two-year degrees related to STEM, completion of STEM graduate programs, and occupational advancement in STEM fields.

Limitations of the Volume

We must also note a few significant limitations of this volume. First, because of space restrictions, we do not discuss the role of gender in the experiences of minority students or the experiences of racial and ethnic minority graduate students. Regarding the former, given that women are also underrepresented in STEM fields (Hanson, 2004; National Science Board, 2002), it is important for future analyses and syntheses of empirical research to consider the unique experiences of women of color because they have distinct experiences and face challenges resulting from a confluence of their racial backgrounds and gender. As for the latter, graduate STEM education is an important aspect of the STEM circuit, and perhaps others will build on this work to review the experiences and outcomes of racial and ethnic minority graduate students in STEM, but such analysis is beyond the scope of this volume.

Another limitation worth noting is that most of our discussion of factors influencing the experiences of racial and ethnic minority students in STEM in college is based on research conducted at four-year colleges and universities—because the vast majority of research on minority students in STEM is conducted on four-year campuses. Nevertheless, two-year colleges represent a critical juncture in the STEM circuit for many racial and ethnic minority students. Future research on the experiences of minority students in STEM at community colleges is therefore critical, a point to which we return later in the volume.

The Current Condition of Minority Students in STEM

Racial and ethnic disparities in the STEM education circuit have received considerable attention in the K–12 and higher education literature over the past few decades. More than thirty years ago, scholars were discussing the underrepresentation of racial and ethnic minorities and the need for more diversity in STEM fields (Chipman and Thomas, 1987; Kiehl, 1971). Evidence clearly suggests that, since that time, racial disparities have persisted at every juncture in the STEM circuit. We provide an overview of that evidence in this section to delineate the current condition of racial and ethnic minority students in STEM education while paying specific attention to each racial minority group. To describe the current condition of minority students in the K–12 component of the STEM circuit, we use math test scores from K–12 education and math SAT college entrance examinations scores, which—although not necessarily an ideal predictor of success in college—are arguably the most accurate standardized measure of STEM preparation available at the K–12 level. To describe the condition of racial and ethnic minority students in STEM in college, we use STEM degree completion rates and recipients. We also incorporate data from the U.S. Census Bureau to highlight within-race diversity and disparities.

Asian American and Pacific Islander Students

Although "Asian American and Pacific Islanders" is the racial category often employed in the collection and analysis of data, it is important to underscore the problematic nature of this label. The AAPI racial category encompasses more than forty unique ethnic groups. For instance, the term "Asian Americans" includes, but is not limited to, Bangladeshi, Cambodian, Chinese, Filipino, Hmong, (Asian) Indian, Indonesian, Japanese, Korean, Laotian, Malaysian, Pakistani, Sri Lankan, Taiwanese, Thai, and Vietnamese Americans (Museus and Kiang, 2009). The term "Pacific Islanders" includes those who are Native Hawaiian, Guamanian/Chamorro, Samoan, Tongan, and Fijian. The often unquestioned reliance on this racial classification to compare various racial groups' success in education oversimplifies the extreme diversity in this population, hinders the ability of researchers and educators to develop a complex understanding of individuals in this category, fuels race-based exclusion of AAPIs from education research and discourse, inhibits the inclusion of this group in meaningful inquiry that can benefit all students, and reinforces stereotypes of other minority students as academically inferior (Hune, 2002; Kiang, 2002; Museus, 2009; Museus and Chang; 2009; Museus and Kiang, 2009; National Consortium on Asian American and Pacific Islander Research in Education [CARE], 2010; Teranishi, 2010). We note that, despite the problematic nature of the AAPI category, we use it throughout this volume because almost all of the extant research on racial and ethnic minorities in STEM employs this or a similar umbrella term and lumps members of this diverse group into one category. We urge readers to interpret statistics presented herein and elsewhere with caution, however, and recognize that the aggregate performance of a racial group is not characteristic of all subgroups or individuals in it.

Indeed, although aggregated statistics consistently suggest that AAPIs succeed at levels higher than any other racial group at all levels of the STEM circuit (see Figures 2 through 8), scholars have repeatedly noted that such analyses mask the broad diversity in the larger racial category and shown that many ethnic groups in that population suffer from drastic racial and ethnic disparities in education (College Board, 2008; Goel, 2006; Hune, 2002; Kiang, 2002; Museus, 2009; Museus, forthcoming; Museus and Kiang, 2009). Indeed, aggregated analyses do not take into account different rates of educational success across ethnic groups in the AAPI population, varying levels of success between Asian Americans and Pacific Islanders, or different levels of success between Asian international and Asian American students. For example, some Asian American ethnic subgroups such as Indian Americans

(63.9 percent) attain bachelor's degrees at over twice the rate of the national population (24.4 percent), while others, including Cambodian (9.2 percent), Hmong (7.5 percent), and Laotian (7.7 percent) Americans, earn four-year degrees at less than half the rate of the national population (see Figure 9). Similarly, although only 8.9 percent of Japanese Americans never earned a high school diploma, that figure is much larger for Hmong (59.6 percent), Cambodian (53.3 percent), and Laotian (49.6 percent) Americans. It is also clear that *all* groups of Pacific Islanders suffer from racial and ethnic disparities in educational attainment, with some groups, including Fijians (8.8 percent), Marshallese (5.1 percent), and Tongans (8.6 percent), holding bachelor's degrees at as low as one-third, or lower than one-third, the rate of the national population (24.4 percent) (Figure 10). Therefore, generalizations of all AAPIs as inherently academically superior are actually a function of racial stereotypes, such as the model minority myth that inaccurately portrays all members of this racial group as achieving universal educational and occupational success, and inadequate statistical analyses rather than a consequence of authentic or intricate understandings of this population (Museus, 2009; Museus and Kiang, 2009).

Just as analyses of general educational attainment rates repeatedly portray AAPIs as a relatively successful homogenous group (see, for example, National Center for Education Statistics, 2007, 2010b), so do examinations of progress and success among AAPIs specifically in STEM fields (American Council on Education, 2006; Babco, 2005; Elliott and others, 1996; National Action Council for Minorities in Engineering, 2008). For example, AAPIs earned 9.3 percent of all bachelor's degrees in science and engineering in 2006, which was much larger than their share of the national population (4.6 percent) in that same year (see Figure 8). Unfortunately, however, such statistics also ignore ethnic differences, even though we know significant variations in educational attainment exist in this population, as well as differences between Asian American and Asian international students. Such statistics also reinforce notions of universal success among AAPIs and lead to their exclusion from meaningful discourse around diversity in STEM (Lee, 1997). This fact is particularly problematic because AAPIs face significant challenges: cultural adjustment difficulties, language barriers, immense pressure from the model minority

Figure 2
Average Fourth-Grade Math Scores by Race

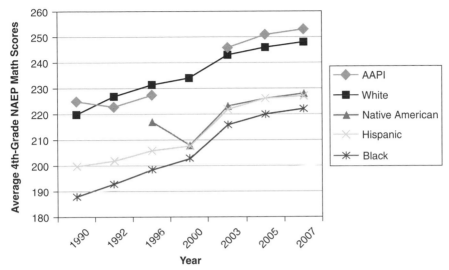

Source: National Assessment of Educational Progress, 2010.

Figure 3
Average Eighth-Grade Math Scores by Race

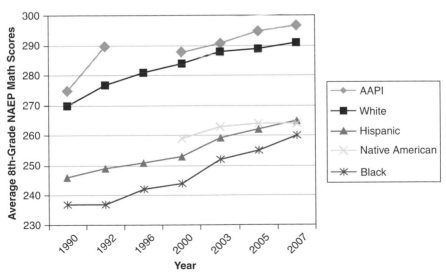

Source: National Assessment of Educational Progress, 2010.

Figure 4
Gains in Fourth- and Eighth-Grade Math Scores from 1990 to 2007 by Race

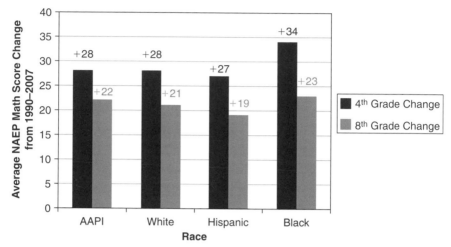

Source: National Assessment of Educational Progress, 2010.

Figure 5
SAT Math Scores by Race

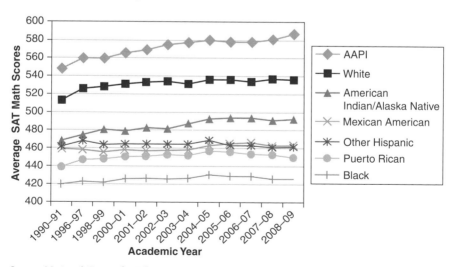

Source: National Center for Education Statistics, 2010a.

Figure 6
Change in SAT Math Scores by Race from 1990–91 to 2008–09

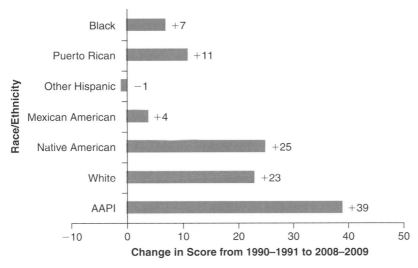

Source: National Center for Education Statistics, 2010a.

Figure 7
STEM Degree Aspirants in 2004 Who Completed STEM Bachelor's Degrees by 2009 by Race

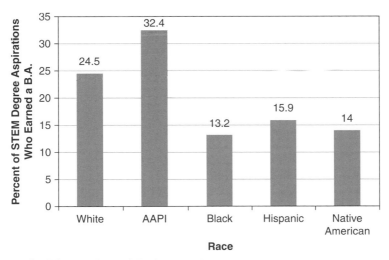

Source: Higher Education Research Institute, 2010.

Figure 8
Proportion of the National Population and Earned Science and Engineering Degrees by Race in 2006

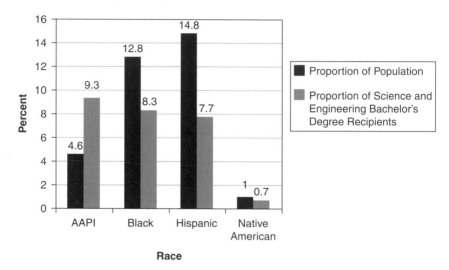

Source: National Science Foundation, 2010b.

Figure 9
Percentage of Each Asian American Ethnic Group, Age 25 and Older, with Less than a High School Diploma or at Least a Bachelor's Degree by Ethnicity

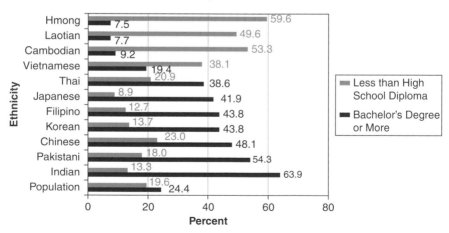

Source: U.S. Census Bureau, 2004b.

Figure 10
Percentage of Each Pacific Islander Ethnic Group, Age 25 and Older, with Less than a High School Diploma or at Least a Bachelor's Degree by Ethnicity

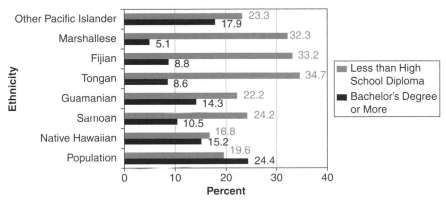

Source: U.S. Census Bureau, 2004e.

stereotype, racial prejudice and discrimination, impoverished and underresourced communities, and a lack of support on college campuses (Chou and Feagin, 2008; Cress and Ikeda, 2003; Hune, 2002; Kiang, 2002; Lewis, Chesler, and Forman, 2000; Maramba, 2008a, 2008b; Museus, 2009; Museus and Kiang, 2009; Ngo and Lee, 2007; Palmer, 2010a).

Given these realities, it is important to include AAPIs in discussions of diversity and minority student success in STEM for at least three primary reasons. First, it is reasonable to question whether various Asian American ethnic groups succeed in STEM at rates higher than other racial groups, but statistics on various groups in the AAPI racial category are not even available to answer such questions. It has been noted, however, that disaggregated analyses can shed light on exaggerated claims of AAPI success in STEM fields. Goel (2006), for example, reported that, although AAPIs are often viewed as omnipresent in mathematics, only about 30 statistics doctoral degrees were awarded to members of this racial group in 2004, and he asserts that Asian Americans are still invisible in many mathematics departments across the nation.

Second, it is unwise to exclude any entire racial group from discussions about how to foster success among diverse populations, particularly when that racial group shares common characteristics (such as racial and ethnic minority status) with populations that are underrepresented. Indeed, Fullilove and Treisman (1990) have demonstrated that a better understanding of AAPIs can lead to more effective efforts at increasing success rates among all students. They observed that Chinese Americans succeeded in math at much higher rates than their Black peers because they studied in groups, which led to the integration of those students' academic and social lives, more time spent studying, and increased peer support. The researchers subsequently created a STEM program designed to foster success among students from all races through the cultivation of communities of learning modeled after the Chinese American peer groups. Third, it is important to acknowledge that persistence through the circuit does not always equal success (Museus and Kiang, 2009). In fact, success can be measured by many other indicators, including development, satisfaction, or occupational advancement. According to some of these measures, AAPIs succeed at lower rates than other groups. For example, they are less satisfied with the college experience than their Hispanic and White peers (Kuh, 2005). AAPIs in STEM majors are also the least satisfied of all racial groups with their chosen field (Grandy, 1994). Finally, evidence exists that AAPIs face a glass ceiling in the STEM workforce and do not succeed at rates equal to White and other minority professionals in STEM occupations (Chen and Farr, 2007; Takei and Sakamoto, 2008; Tang, 1993).

In sum, racial stereotypes and aggregated race-based statistical analyses continue to dominate scholarly research and discourse on AAPIs in STEM fields. Although disaggregated analyses do suggest that ethnic diversity exists in the AAPI population, some Asian American and Pacific Islander ethnic groups suffer from disparities in educational attainment, AAPIs face important challenges, and current national data are inadequate for constructing a clear picture of the current condition of various AAPI ethnic groups.

Black Students

Just as diversity exists in the AAPI racial group, the Black American population is also heterogeneous. Unlike many AAPIs, however, the vast majority of Blacks were born into families that have been in the United States for generations.

In fact, approximately 94 percent of the Black population is native born (U.S. Census Bureau, 2004c). Among Blacks who are foreign born, individuals hail from Africa (24.4 percent), Asia (0.8 percent), the Caribbean (59.6 percent), and Central and South America (11.9 percent). Despite the presence of these different groups, the STEM education literature contains no discussion of this within-race ethnic diversity.

As noted earlier, Black students suffer from racial disparities in the education system in general. For example, most recent statistics indicate that about 42 percent of Black students who matriculate at a four-year postsecondary institution complete a baccalaureate degree within six years, which is approximately 18 percent lower than their White peers (National Center for Education Statistics, 2007). Black students have been the focus of scholarly discourse around minority student success in STEM fields for more than two decades because they suffer from racial disparities in the STEM circuit as well. In 1990, for example, Anderson underscored the disparities faced by Blacks in STEM fields when he reported that, although they accounted for 12 percent of the national population, Blacks constituted only about 2 percent of the nation's scientists and engineers. Unfortunately, this population continues to suffer from racial disparities at every level of the STEM circuit.

The racial disparities from which Blacks suffer appear to begin very early in the education system. According to nationwide fourth-grade math scores, Black students exhibit the lowest levels of performance of all racial groups (Figure 2). This disparity continues into the eighth grade (Figure 3). As shown in Figure 4, Black students did make the most gains in both fourth- and eighth-grade math achievement between 1990 and 2007. Nevertheless, their eighth-grade math scores continued to trail those of all other racial groups. Statistics indicate that Blacks also exhibit the lowest SAT math scores of all racial groups (Figure 5). Between the 1990–91 and 2008–09 academic years, however, Black SAT math scores increased seven points, which was a greater gain than Mexican Americans (four) and Other Hispanics (minus one) but smaller than Puerto Ricans (eleven), Native Americans (twenty-five), Whites (twenty-three), and AAPIs (thirty-nine) (Figure 6).

These racial disparities continue into higher education. Empirical evidence from the Higher Education Research Institute (2010) indicate that, when

STEM degree aspirants' rates of degree completion are broken down by race, Black students who aspire to attain a STEM degree have the lowest rates of completion among all racial groups. Specifically, 13.2 percent of Black STEM degree aspirants complete a STEM degree within five years of matriculation, compared with 14 percent of Native Americans, 15.9 percent of Hispanics, 24.5 percent of Whites, and 32.4 percent of AAPIs. Moreover, Blacks receive a noticeably low proportion of science and engineering bachelor's degrees (8.3 percent), compared with their share of the national population (12.8 percent).

In sum, statistics consistently indicate that Black students' success in the STEM circuit trails that of all other racial groups. This finding holds true from elementary school math achievement through college degree completion. Moreover, although signs of progress exist for this group, the racial and ethnic disparities that have plagued many groups of color in STEM persist. Thus, it is imperative that educational researchers, policymakers, and practitioners continue to better understand how they can foster success among this population.

Hispanic Students

Similar to other racial designations, the Hispanic label encompasses individuals from a wide range of cultures and ethnic origins. Specifically, this group includes people with origins in Mexico, Puerto Rico, Cuba, Central America, South America, the Dominican Republic, and Spain (U.S. Census Bureau, 2004d). Also, much like for their AAPI counterparts, disparities in educational attainment appear across ethnic groups in the Hispanic population. For example, 29.9 percent of Spaniards and 25.2 percent of South Americans hold a baccalaureate degree, which is higher than the rate of the national population (24.4 percent), but those of Puerto Rican (12.5 percent), Dominican (10.9 percent), Central American (9.5 percent), and Mexican (7.5 percent) origins attain four-year degrees at half, or less than half, the rate of the national population (see Figure 11). Thus, we echo our earlier assertions in the section on AAPIs about the importance of moving beyond simplistic aggregated analyses to more complex understandings of the experiences and outcomes of various ethnic groups. We also need to understand better the ethnic disparities in the Hispanic population at various levels of the STEM education circuit.

Figure 11
Percentage of Each Hispanic Ethnic Group, Age 25 and Older, with Less than a High School Diploma or at Least a Bachelor's Degree by Ethnicity

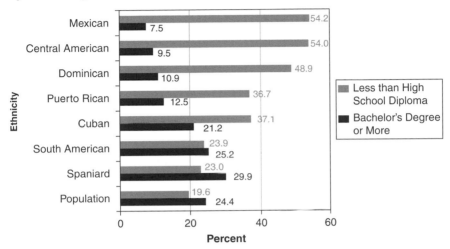

Source: U.S. Census Bureau, 2004d.

Few analyses, however, disaggregate the Hispanic category. In the aggregate, statistics indicate that Hispanic students also suffer from major racial disparities at all levels of the STEM circuit. Not only do Hispanic students exhibit fourth- and eighth-grade achievement levels below their AAPI and White peers but they also appear to be making the smallest gains in math achievement at those grade levels, according to statistics from 1990 to 2007 (see Figures 2 through 5). On the math component of the SAT, Hispanics also perform at lower levels than their AAPI, White, and Native American peers, which is a trend that persisted from 1990 to 2007.

Interestingly, SAT math scores have been disaggregated into three subgroups—Puerto Rican, Mexican, and Other Hispanic—allowing for some analyses of disparities in this population. In most recent years, it appears that Puerto Rican students score slightly lower on the SAT math test than Mexican and Other Hispanic students. In addition with regard to changes in SAT math scores from 1990 to 2007, disparities exist in progress made across Hispanic subgroups. Although Puerto Ricans (11 percent) made greater gains than their Black peers

(7 percent) over those seventeen years, Mexican (4 percent) and Other Hispanic (–1 percent) students demonstrated the smallest gains (Figure 6). In terms of both recent scores and gains in scores between 1990 and 2007, however, all three Hispanic groups fared worse than their AAPI and White peers.

Hispanic students also exhibit lower levels of success than their AAPI and White counterparts in higher education. For example, 48 percent of Hispanic students who matriculate at a four-year institution will complete a bachelor's degree within six years of matriculation, which is approximately 12 percent lower than their White counterparts (National Center for Education Statistics, 2010b). Statistics focused specifically on STEM fields indicate that 15.9 percent of Hispanic students who aspire to attain a STEM degree accomplish that goal. This figure is slightly higher than for Blacks (13.2 percent) and Native Americans (14 percent) but substantially lower than for AAPI (24.5 percent) and White (32.4 percent) students (Figure 7). Moreover, empirical evidence suggests that Hispanics remain severely underrepresented among STEM graduates (Figure 8). Although they accounted for approximately 14.8 percent of the national population in 2006, they earned only 7.7 percent of bachelor's degrees conferred in the fields of science and engineering. This gap is the largest one between proportion of the national population and earned degrees among all racial groups.

In sum, the Hispanic racial category consists of diverse ethnic populations, and disparities in educational attainment exist across these groups. Most research, however, aggregates these populations in analyses of student success in STEM. These analyses show that Hispanics, while achieving at higher levels than Blacks on some measures, have suffered and continue to suffer from inequities at all levels of the STEM circuit. That evidence also shows that Hispanic students appear to be making fewer gains than other racial groups in math achievement throughout the K–12 education system. Given that it is the fastest-growing racial group in the United States, the relative lack of progress among this group is most troubling. Perhaps the lack of progress is a function of a reluctance of educators to invest in the potential talent of Hispanic students (Rochin and Mello, 2007). Therefore, it is critical that K–12 and postsecondary educators take seriously the importance of fostering success among this population.

Native American Students

Native Americans are also a diverse population; they include more than 560 tribes recognized by the federal government (Babco, 2005): the Apache, Cherokee, Chippewa, Choctaw, Creek, Iroquois, Lumbee, Navajo, Pueblo, and Sioux as well as Alaskan Native groups such as the Alaskan Athabascan, Aleut, Eskimo, and Tlingit-Haida (U.S. Census Bureau, 2004a). Native Americans make up approximately 1 percent of the national population—1.5 percent of the nation when multiracial Native Americans are included. Both aggregated and disaggregated empirical evidence indicate that all of these ethnic subpopulations face racial and ethnic disparities in attaining general education.

Some indicators of educational progress might appear promising for Native Americans (Babco, 2005), but most evidence clearly indicates that this population continues to suffer from racial disparities. Regarding STEM-specific achievement, although Native Americans perform better than Black students on fourth- and eighth-grade assessments of mathematical skills, they trail significantly behind their AAPI and White peers (Figures 2 and 3). In addition, since 2003 this gap appears to have widened. Native Americans' scores on the SAT math test are better than their Black and Hispanic counterparts, and Native Americans' scores on this examination increased more than those of most other racial groups between the 1990–91 and 2008–09 academic years (Figure 6). Nevertheless, Native Americans' performance on the SAT math test still lags far behind their AAPI and White peers (Figure 5).

According to national statistics, however, aside from Hispanics, Native Americans continue to have the lowest rates of high school and four-year college degree completion (Babco, 2005). Among students who matriculate at a four-year institution, for example, Native Americans have the lowest timely degree completion rate among all racial groups (National Center for Education Statistics, 2010b). For those who aspire to attain STEM degrees specifically, it is apparent that Native Americans (14 percent) fare only slightly better than Blacks (13.2 percent) and slightly worse than Hispanics (15.9 percent) but trail substantially behind AAPIs (67 percent) and Whites (60 percent). Some studies indicate that Native Americans are underrepresented among those earning science and engineering degrees. In 2006, for example, they earned less than 0.7 percent of science and engineering degrees but accounted for 1 percent of the national population.

In sum, although some indicators suggest that the success of Native Americans in STEM has improved, they still suffer from major disparities. Native Americans perform better than Blacks on early math assessments and better than Blacks and Hispanics on SAT math exam scores, but on every measure of STEM success, from fourth-grade math tests to bachelor's degree completion in STEM fields, Native Americans fare substantially worse than AAPIs and Whites. Thus, Native Americans continue to be an untapped resource for STEM educators.

The Impact of Race and Racism on Minority Students' Success in STEM

Before reviewing existing literature that examines the various factors that contribute to and hinder success among racial and ethnic minority students in STEM education, it is essential to underscore the role of race and racism in this discussion for three reasons. First, we believe that any discussion based on racially and ethnically disadvantaged students implies that race and racism are central to understanding those individuals' experiences. Indeed, the racial inequalities that exist throughout the STEM education circuit and the nature of those disparities cannot be understood fully without acknowledging that race and racism play a critical role in the experiences of minority students.

Second, although researchers have rarely discussed the role of race and racism in minority students' experiences and outcomes in STEM explicitly, we highlight the fact that the salience of race and racism are embedded implicitly throughout that discussion. The following chapter on K–12 education, for example, illuminates several ways that the racial oppression of minority students manifests itself in the education system, including unequal funding systems in K–12 education, the perpetuation of a reliance on White Eurocentric curricula, and culturally pervasive and harmful racial stereotypes. Likewise, "Factors in K–12 Education That Influence Success Among Racial and Ethnic Minority College Students in the STEM Circuit" discusses how oppressive and culturally biased meritocratic structures, campus cultures based on White European individualistic values, marginalizing predominantly White campus cultures, and racial prejudice and discrimination in the campus climate influence minority students in STEM.

Third, race and racism constitute a useful framework for understanding the condition, experience, and outcomes of racial and ethnic minority students. Researchers, for example, have used Critical Race Theory (CRT) to make sense of racial and ethnic minority students' experiences and outcomes in education (for in-depth discussion, see Dixson and Rousseau, 2006; Taylor, Gillborn, and Ladson-Billings, 2009). CRT challenges notions of colorblindness, merit, and racial equality and can be used to elucidate the inequitable distribution of power and privilege that exists throughout society and social institutions (Bell, 1987; Crenshaw, Gotanda, Peller, and Thomas, 1995; Delgado and Stefancic, 2001). If racial exclusion is a part of the cultural fabric of American educational institutions (Taylor, 2000), CRT emphasizes the ways by which pervasive institutional policies and practices perpetuate racial inequity in the education system (Villalpando, 2004). Thus, we urge readers to keep in mind that race and racism throughout larger society, the education system, and in social interactions are central to understanding racial disparities and minority students' success throughout all stages of the STEM circuit.

Factors in K–12 Education That Influence the Success of Racial and Ethnic Minority Students in the STEM Circuit

R ESEARCH SHOWS THAT SEVERAL FACTORS in kindergarten through grade 12 hinder or contribute to racial and ethnic minority students' success in the STEM circuit. One central factor that limits their success in the STEM circuit is their inadequate levels of academic preparation for college (Anderson, 1996; Astin and Astin, 1992; Bonous-Hammarth, 2006; Chang, Cerna, Han, and Sàenz, 2008; Denson, Avery, and Schell, 2010; Fenske, Porter, and DuBrock, 2000; Grandy, 1998; Maple and Stage, 1991; Moore, 2006; National Science Foundation, 2006; Seymour and Hewitt, 1997). Moreover, a number of factors in K–12 contribute to racial and ethnic minority students' lack of academic preparedness for college level work in STEM (Bonous-Hammarth, 2006; Denson, Avery, and Schell, 2010; Grandy, 1998; Hrabowski and Maton, 1995; Lewis, 2003; May and Chubin, 2003; Moore, 2006; Seymour and Hewitt, 1997). Beyond academic preparation, however, several other precollege variables influence racial and ethnic minority students' success in STEM.

This chapter synthesizes factors in K–12 that restrict and promote racial and ethnic minority students' success in the STEM circuit. Specifically, three questions guided this chapter: What factors in K–12 hinder the success of racial and ethnic minority students in the STEM circuit? What factors in K–12 contribute to the success of racial and ethnic minority students in the STEM circuit? What initiatives in K–12 have been implemented to foster the success of racial and ethnic minority students in the STEM circuit?

We synthesize existing research to address each of these questions successively. The first section briefly discusses the critical connection between academic preparedness in K–12 and success in the STEM circuit, the second highlights factors in K–12 contributing to the insufficient academic preparation among racial and ethnic minority students in STEM education, and the third identifies factors in K–12 that contribute to the success of racial and ethnic minority students in the STEM circuit. The final section describes initiatives implemented in K–12 to help increase the success of racial and ethnic minority students in the STEM education circuit.

The Link Between Academic Preparedness in K–12 Education and Minority Students' Success in STEM

A preponderance of research illustrates that success in the STEM circuit is based on adequate academic preparation for college-level work in STEM (Bonous-Hammarth, 2000, 2006; Denson, Avery, and Schell, 2010; Grandy, 1998; Hall and Post-Kammer, 1987; Oakes, 1990; Rendón and Triana, 1989). Specifically, the mathematics and science courses that students take before college determine who will receive further training in STEM fields (Anderson, 1996; Astin and Astin, 1992; Chang, Cerna, Han, and Sàenz, 2008; Denson, Avery, and Schell, 2010; Fenske, Porter, and DuBrock, 2000; Maple and Stage, 1991; Maton, Hrabowski, and Schmitt, 2000; National Science Foundation, 2006). For example, using data from the National Education Longitudinal Study (NELS: 88/00), which sampled more than twelve thousand students in eighth grade and tracked them for twelve years, Adelman (2006) found that the academic intensity of students' high school curriculum was a more powerful predictor of their ability to complete the baccalaureate degree than any other precollege factor.

Despite the salient connection between academic preparation in K–12 and success in the STEM circuit, research shows the enrollment of Blacks, Hispanics, and Native Americans is limited in mathematics and science courses in K–12 (Bonous-Hammarth, 2000, 2006; Hrabowski and Maton, 1995; Maton, Hrabowski, and Schmitt, 2000; Moore, 2006; Seymour and Hewitt, 1997; Rendón and Triana, 1989; Simpson, 2001). Bonous-Hammarth (2000), who examined a nationally representative sample using cross tabulations, factor analyses, and logistic regressions, found that Black, Hispanic, and Native American undergraduates were less likely to be retained in science, mathematics, and engineering majors in college compared with their White and AAPI counterparts because they were inadequately prepared in K–12 to succeed in these subjects. A study of women and racial and ethnic minority students in STEM concluded that "one cannot understand why . . . minorities are underrepresented in science and engineering unless one understands that the related behaviors are formed . . . in the years prior to college. Although collegiate interventions . . . can increase minority students' participation rates, the critical damage is done much earlier" (Leslie, McClure, and Oaxaca, 1998, p. 268).

The next section discusses the variables that hinder racial and ethnic minority students' academic preparedness for college-level work in STEM.

K–12 Contributors to the Insufficient Academic Preparation of Minority Students in STEM

As discussed, research indicates that insufficient academic preparation among minority students in science and mathematics in K–12 education is tightly coupled to their lack of success in the STEM education circuit. Accordingly, this section highlights eight factors in K–12 that contribute to the inadequate academic preparation of racial and ethnic minority students in STEM: (1) school district funding disparities, (2) tracking into remedial courses, (3) underrepresentation in Advanced Placement courses, (4) unqualified teachers, (5) low teacher expectations, (6) stereotype threat, (7) oppositional culture, and (8) premature departure from high school.

School District Funding Disparities

One factor that contributes to the underpreparedness of racial and ethnic minority students in the STEM circuit is disparities in school funding (Adelman, 2006; Flores, 2007; Oakes, 1990). In many cases, schools are funded through local property taxes. Thus, schools in more affluent neighborhoods receive more funding per pupil than schools in less wealthy communities, putting Blacks, Hispanics, and low-income students at a disadvantage because they are more likely to live in inner cities and underresourced communities. For example, data from the National Assessment of Educational Progress (NAEP) show that, although 3 percent of White eighth graders are in schools where more than 75 percent of the students qualify for free or reduced lunch, 35 percent of eighth-grade Blacks and 34 percent of Hispanics are in such schools (Flores, 2007). As a result of this funding system and the fact that many racial and ethnic minorities are more likely to come from less affluent communities, school districts that serve a large number of Blacks and Hispanics receive less local and state funding to educate students compared with school districts that serve a low percentage of racial and ethnic minority students (De La Cruz, 1998; Fergus, 2009; Flores, 2007; Gándara and Contreras, 2009; Rendón and Hope, 1996; Wilkins and Education Trust, 2006). Although we do not have access to these data for Southeast Asian American and Pacific Islander students because they suffer from major economic disparities (U.S. Census Bureau, 2004b, 2004e), we can hypothesize that these groups also disproportionately attend schools that suffer from such funding disparities.

The funding disparity between school districts is tightly coupled with the kind of resources their schools are able to provide for students. For example, schools with more resources are able to offer smaller classes, which positively contribute to students' learning and achievement (Wenglinsky, 1997). This situation puts racial and ethnic minority students at a disadvantage, given that they disproportionately attend schools with fewer resources and therefore larger classes. Moreover, because racial and ethnic minority students attend K–12 schools that receive less funding, these schools typically are not able to provide the latest books, laboratories, instructional material, and technology compared with those that receive more funding (May and Chubin, 2003). According to May and Chubin, the disparity in school funding also engenders a digital divide, further impairing racial and ethnic minority students' ability to succeed in mathematics and science (Rendón and Hope, 1996).

Tracking into Remedial Courses
Another systemic factor that contributes to the disproportionate underpreparedness of racial and ethnic minority students is academic tracking. Academic tracking can be defined as the schools' systematic placement of students

in classes based on their performance on standardized testing or teachers' perception of their academic ability (Oakes, Gamoran, and Page, 1992). Such tracking promotes racial and ethnic inequality because students who are placed in high-achieving academic tracks are exposed to more complex and challenging classroom instruction than those who are placed in low-achieving academic tracks. For example, Gamoran, Porter, Smithson, and White (1997) conducted a quantitative study using data from school districts in San Francisco and San Diego, California, and Rochester and Buffalo, New York. The researchers selected these districts because they were urban districts with a high percentage of low-achieving students and had recently implemented new mathematics initiatives. Using a three-level hierarchical model, they found that students in high-achieving academic tracks learned more than students in low-achieving academic tracks. To this end, the authors concluded, "General-track math classes should be eliminated. Instruction is weak, achievement is shallow, and general math is a dead end for students' mathematics careers" (p. 333).

Moreover, existing empirical research shows that Blacks and Hispanics are overrepresented in low-ability or remedial tracks (Bonous-Hammarth, 2006; Oakes, 1990, 1995; Simpson, 2001; Tyson, Lee, Borman, and Hanson, 2007), even when their scores on standardized assessments are equal to or better than those of their White peers (Gándara, 2006; Flores, 2007; Oakes, 1995). Indeed, in a comprehensive review of the literature on women and racial and ethnic minority students in science and mathematics, Oakes (1990) noted that Blacks and Hispanics are tracked into remedial courses in elementary schools, which subsequently makes it difficult for them to succeed in mathematics and science courses as they advance through the education system. Although no information is readily available regarding the tracking of Southeast Asian Americans, Xiong (2010) has argued that those students may be disproportionately channeled into remedial tracks in K–12 schools and that such tracking negatively influences their future choices regarding postsecondary education as well. Because tracking hinders minority students' ability to learn advanced science and mathematics and may negatively influence their college choices, it is an important barrier to educational equity (Tate, 1995b).

Underrepresentation in Advanced Placement Courses

Although racial and ethnic minority students are overrepresented in remedial courses, they are underrepresented in Advanced Placement (AP) courses (May and Chubin, 2003). Indeed, Adelman (2006), using nationally representative data, provided evidence of the disparity in access to AP courses suffered by racial and ethnic minority students. Specifically, he found that, compared with White or AAPI students, Hispanics are far less likely to attend high schools that offer AP courses in subjects such as trigonometry and calculus. Similarly, Ladson-Billings (1997) explains that schools that disproportionately serve a large number of Black students tend to have "less demanding mathematics programs and offer fewer opportunities for students to take such gatekeeper courses as algebra and calculus that lead to increased opportunities at the college level and beyond" (p. 701). This underrepresentation in AP courses is important because college preparatory coursework has a positive impact on a variety of achievement outcomes such as higher scores on standardized college entrance assessments and is tied to more completed years of education (Bonous-Hammarth, 2006; Fergus, 2009). Thus, the underrepresentation of Blacks and Hispanics—and possibly Southeast Asian Americans—in AP courses negatively influences their preparation and subsequent success (Solórzano and Ornelas, 2004; Xiong, 2010).

Even when Advanced Placement courses in mathematics and science are available, many minority students do not engage in them for several reasons (Clewell, Anderson, and Thorpe, 1992). First, racial and ethnic minority students do not view these courses as relevant to their future educational and career trajectories. Second, many minority students view courses in advanced mathematics and science as difficult and do not believe it is worth investing additional time to do well in them. Indeed, although Blacks plan to pursue scientific careers in numbers similar to Whites, because they are not adequately prepared academically, they abandon their pursuit of science careers once they start to encounter more challenging courses (Lewis, 2003). Third, math anxiety can cause racial and ethnic minority students to avoid participating in advanced mathematics and science courses. Finally, perhaps the most critical cause of the underrepresentation of racial and ethnic minority students in AP courses is their elementary and junior high school experiences. That is, because a disproportionate percentage of Blacks and Hispanics have been placed in remedial or general mathematics and science tracks, they are ill prepared to succeed in more rigorous mathematics and science courses in high school and beyond.

Unqualified Teachers

The underrepresentation of qualified teachers among educators who serve large numbers of racial and ethnic minority students is another contributor to their lack of academic preparedness in STEM. A report from the National Science Foundation (2010c) underscores the severity of racial and ethnic minority students' not having equal access to qualified teachers in mathematics and science. For example, the report noted that, in 2004, White fifth graders were 51 percent more likely to be taught by teachers with a master's or advanced degree than their Black and Hispanic peers. Similarly, Flores (2007) and others (for example, Bissell, 2000; Darling-Hammond, 2000; Fergus, 2009; Ladson-Billings, 1997; Tate, 2008) have explained that students attending predominantly Black and Hispanic schools are twice as likely to be taught by teachers with three years of teaching experience or less, compared with those attending predominantly White schools.

Although the overexposure to unqualified teachers is a racial issue, it is also a socioeconomic one. According to Mayer, Mullens, and Moore (2000), the percentage of teachers in high-poverty schools who are inexperienced is 20 percent, compared with 11 percent of those at low-poverty schools. In addition, Flores (2007) noted that, whereas out-of-field teachers teach 19 percent of classes in low-poverty schools, that figure is 34 percent in high-poverty schools. Flores also explains that the least-prepared teachers are disproportionately found in underresourced schools populated by low-income racial and ethnic minority students from inner cities and rural communities. Because a disproportionate number of racial and ethnic minority students are deprived of access to qualified mathematics teachers, which hinders achievement and limits their participation in key aspects of the knowledge-based economy, efforts to provide ways for them to become literate in mathematics is a civil rights issue (Schoenfeld, 2002).

Evidence regarding the impact of teacher preparation on student outcomes is generally consistent in its indication that teacher qualifications in the subject they teach does, in fact, affect success among all students in the STEM education circuit. A majority of existing research on this topic suggests that students who are taught by individuals with a degree in the subject are more likely to have more positive educational outcomes (Goldhaber and Brewer, 1997a, 1997b, 2000; Hill, Rowan, and Ball, 2005; Monk, 1994; Rowan, Chiang, and Miller, 1997). For example, using data from the NELS, Goldhaber and Brewer (2000) used multiple regression techniques to examine the relationship between teacher subject certification and students' academic achievement. Their results revealed that math students who were instructed by teachers with baccalaureate or master's degrees in mathematics had higher test scores compared with students who were taught by teachers with out-of-subject degrees.

Low Teacher Expectations

In addition to unqualified teachers, teachers' low expectations can hinder the achievement of racial and ethnic minority students in math and science courses (Bissell, 2000; Collins, 1992; Fergus, 2009; Oakes, 1990; Thompson, Warren, and Carter, 2004). Moreover, the relationship between teachers' expectations and academic achievement appears to be a reciprocal one. That is, although teachers' expectations influence academic achievement, students' academic performance can also affect teachers' expectations of those pupils. Indeed, teachers may be more likely to develop expectations about and treat their students in a manner that is more consistent with those students' performance on standardized assessments than their actual abilities (Thompson, Warren, and Carter, 2004). Thus, given that racial and ethnic minority students are likely to perform lower on standardized math and science examinations than their majority counterparts (see the first chapter), teachers are more likely to have higher expectations for White than minority students.

In turn, research demonstrates that teachers' expectations can influence academic performance, suggesting that those expectations can become a self-fulfilling prophecy for students. More specifically, mathematics and science courses are viewed as higher-order disciplines, and teachers are inclined to perceive racial and ethnic minority students as lacking ability in those areas and send subtle messages that such disciplines are White male domains (Clewell, Anderson, and Thorpe, 1992). Moreover, such messages can lead to differences in teaching behavior and subsequent achievement (Bissell, 2000). In addition, racial and ethnic minority students in particular seem to be influenced by what they believe teachers think of them and their ability to succeed in mathematics and science courses (Clewell, Anderson, and Thorpe, 1992).

It is important to note that, although existing research shows that teachers' expectations can have a negative impact on the academic success of racial and ethnic minority students in STEM, it also indicates that caring teachers can have a positive impact on the academic preparedness and success of racial and ethnic minority students in those fields (Brown, 2002; Fries-Britt, Younger, and Hall, 2010). For example, using in-depth qualitative interview methods, Brown (2002) examined the experiences of twenty-two Hispanic students majoring in engineering to understand the factors that affected their academic success and found that caring and kind teachers in K–12 played a critical role in their academic achievement in college.

Stereotype Threat

Closely related to negative teacher perceptions and low teacher expectations is the concept of stereotype threat. Stereotype threat has been defined as "a situational threat—a threat in the air—that, in general form, can affect the members of any group about whom a negative stereotype exists. Where bad stereotypes about these groups apply, members of these groups can fear being reduced to that stereotype. And for those who identify with the domain to which the stereotype is relevant, this predicament can be self-threatening" (Steele, 1999, p. 614). Although stereotype threat is often associated with Black students, research has shown that it is applicable to several groups in both K–12 and higher education settings (see, for example, Aronson, Quinn, and Spencer, 1998; Good, Aronson, and Inzlicht, 2003; Spencer, Steele, and Quinn, 1999; Steele and Aronson, 1995). For example, research shows that stereotype threat may account for the academic outcomes of females in mathematic courses (Inzlicht and Ben-Zeev, 2000; Good, Aronson, and Harder, 1999), students from low socioeconomic status (Croizet and Claire, 1998), and any groups for whom stigma has been imposed on their intellectual ability (Aronson and others, 1999). Thus, stereotype threat can be one of the factors implicated for the academic outcomes for minorities in STEM education.

Several studies have developed and tested interventions that may ameliorate the negative effects of stereotype threats (Aronson, Fried, and Good, 2002; Good, Aronson, and Inzlicht, 2003; Wilson and Linville, 1985). Good, Aronson, and Inzlicht, for example, randomly assigned 138 seventh-grade students (63 percent Hispanic, 15 percent Black, and 22 percent White) to four groups that were mentored by college students to determine whether their mentoring intervention would ameliorate the threat of gender stereotypes and reduce the gender gap in mathematics test scores in the sample. The first treatment group learned about the expandable nature of intelligence. The second treatment group learned that everyone encountered difficulty when initially transitioning into seventh grade but that things would improve. In the third treatment group, students learned the combination of the first two messages. These three groups were compared with the fourth, or control, group. At the end of the school year, students completed a statewide standardized test in mathematics and reading. Using analysis of variance tests, Good, Aronson, and Inzlicht discerned that, in all three experimental groups, the gender gap disappeared. Although not specifically focused on racial stereotypes, Good, Aronson, and Inzlicht's intervention (2003) suggests that, although stereotype threat may impede academic progress for racial and ethnic minority students, the effects can be reduced or eliminated with interventions designed to psychologically combat the negative stereotypes. Moreover, these findings are supported by earlier studies (Aronson, Fried, and Good, 2002; Wilson and Linville, 1985). We revisit the impact of stereotype threat later.

One phenomenon related to increased likelihood of stereotype threat is tokenism—being one or one of a few members of an identity group. Indeed, research has found that people are sensitive to being in the minority (Kanter, 1977; Lord and Sàenz, 1985), and being a token can result in increased attention from others and responsibility to represent one's own group (Sàenz, 1994). Scholars have also demonstrated that women who expect to be tokens are more likely to expect to be stereotyped than men (Cohen and Swim, 1995). Although this research focuses on women, we can hypothesize that racial and ethnic minority students in general and in STEM specifically who feel like tokens will feel increased susceptibility to being stereotyped as well, which could make them more vulnerable to stereotype threat.

Oppositional Culture

Researchers have also implicated oppositional culture for the negative academic outcomes of minorities in kindergarten through twelfth grade. Oppositional culture is a theory that Fordham and Ogbu (1986) proposed to explain the academic disengagement of Blacks. The authors explain that Blacks have formed a culture in opposition to mainstream values and norms stemming from the racial oppression, enslavement, and discrimination they have experienced. This oppositional culture acts as a barrier between Blacks and Whites, and it provokes Blacks to persuade their same-race peers to devalue academic success because of its association with "acting White."

Several researchers have raised criticism and concern about oppositional culture as an explanation of the academic disparities faced by Blacks (Ainsworth-Darnell and Downey, 1998; Cook and Ludwig, 1998; Kao and Tienda, 1998; Tyson, Darity, and Castellino, 2005). For example, Cook and Ludwig (1998) argue that Blacks have a desire to attend college, spend an equal amount of time on homework, and have similar rates of absenteeism compared with their White counterparts from the same socioeconomic class. Notwithstanding the criticism, some support does exist for the theory's relevancy in accounting for the disparity in educational outcomes among Blacks (Ford, Grantham, and Whiting, 2008), particularly Black males (Lundy, 2005; Majors and Billson, 1992). Further, using NAEP data collected from students who were fourth graders in 1998, researchers have found that oppositional culture is not limited to Blacks; other racial and ethnic groups experienced oppositional culture as well (Farkas, Lleras, and Maczuga, 2002). For example, the NAEP data revealed that Blacks and Hispanics experienced significantly more oppositional peer culture than Whites. In addition, Native Americans experienced more significant oppositional peer culture than Whites but not to the same degree as Hispanics and Blacks. Although a lot of criticism exists about oppositional culture, this theory could plausibly be used to explain the negative educational outcomes of racial and ethnic minorities in K–12, particularly in STEM education. This literature on oppositional culture highlights the importance of educators and school personnel in K–12 encouraging all students, especially racial and ethnic minority students, to be cognizant of the relationship between peer interaction and academic achievement. We revisit the importance of peers later.

Premature Departure from High School

Finally, premature departure from high school plays a critical role in the inadequate academic preparedness of racial and ethnic minority students in the STEM circuit (Fergus, 2009; Gándara and Contreras, 2009). This situation appears to be particularly salient for Hispanic students who, according to data from Child Trends Databank (2005), exhibit a dropout rate between ages sixteen and twenty-four of 23 percent, while that figure is 11 percent for Blacks and 6 percent for Whites. Given that most careers in STEM require postsecondary training, many Hispanic students miss the chance to even consider a career in STEM because of their departure from the STEM circuit—and the education circuit altogether—in high school (Gándara and Contreras, 2009; Tornatzky, Macias, and Solis, 2006). As we noted in the first chapter, it is also evident that disproportionately large numbers of Southeast Asian Americans and Pacific Islanders also fail to complete high school (Figures 9 and 10).

In summary, research indicates that academic preparedness in K–12 is crucial for the ability of racial and ethnic minorities to be successful in the STEM circuit. Many of those students are insufficiently prepared to succeed in the STEM education circuit, however. To enhance the preparation and success of racial and ethnic minority students in STEM education, it is critical that the factors that negatively affect the success of minority students in K–12 be mitigated. The remaining section of this chapter focuses on variables in K–12 that contribute to the success of racial and ethnic minority students in the STEM circuit.

K–12 Factors That Promote the Success of Minority Students in STEM

Although educational researchers have highlighted the variables in K–12 that hinder the academic preparation of racial and ethnic minority students in STEM, they have also identified six major factors in K–12 that contribute to success among racial and ethnic minority students in the STEM circuit. This section discusses those six variables: (1) parental involvement and support, (2) bilingual education, (3) culturally relevant teaching, (4) early exposure to careers in STEM, (5) interest in STEM subjects, and (6) self-efficacy in STEM domains.

Parental and Support Involvement

A number of researchers have noted that parental expectations and involvement can facilitate the success of racial and ethnic minority students—Black students in particular—in the STEM circuit (Fries-Britt, Younger, and Hall, 2010; Hrabowski, 2003; Hrabowski and Maton, 1995; Russell and Atwater, 2005; Smith and Hausfaus, 1998). Russell and Atwater, for example, interviewed eleven Black college students attending a predominantly White institution (PWI) to gain insight into factors that lead them to pursue and persist in STEM majors. They highlighted the importance of the participants' parents emphasizing the significance of a good education and having high expectations while the students were in primary or secondary schools. Participants also credited their parents for helping them develop good study skills. Similarly, a study that Moore (2006) conducted with forty-two Black males in engineering revealed how the participants' parents affected their desire to pursue engineering in college. Although research underscores the impact of parental expectations and involvement on success among racial and ethnic minority students in STEM in K–12 and higher education, it also shows that parents of Hispanic students may not know how to engage in their children's education (Rendón and Triana, 1989). Therefore, Rendón and Triana recommend that schools provide information to parents of Hispanic students and explain to them why their children are engaged in various mathematics and science courses so they will better understand their children's educational process and how to help them.

Bilingual Education

Researchers have also explained how bilingual instruction in mathematics and science courses can contribute to success among racial and ethnic minority students (for example, AAPI, Hispanic, and Native American) with limited English proficiency in the STEM circuit (see, for example, De La Cruz, 1998; Gándara, 2006; Rendón, 1982; Rendón and Hope, 1996; Rolon, 2003; Rosenthal, 1993). Gándara estimates that at least 50 percent of Hispanic students in California begin school with a language other than English. Consequently, a very large percentage of Hispanic students grapple with understanding English as well as comprehending the curriculum when they enter school. A federally mandated study on student achievement highlighted the importance of language proficiency by underscoring the fact that English learners consistently score lower on achievement tests than other children, even when compared with their counterparts from similar socioeconomic backgrounds (Puma and others, 1997).

Notwithstanding the academic struggles of English learners in school, research indicates that bilingual education facilitates academic success among students with limited English proficiency. According to Rendón and Hope (1996), "Bilingual education . . . [is] considered essential to help students make the successful transition into an English-driven curriculum" (p. 19). Rolon (2003) echoed Rendón and Hope's assertion by discussing how incorporating bilingualism into education positively affects the achievement of Hispanics. In particular, she discussed six high schools in California and Arizona that were successful in enhancing the achievement of Hispanics by including bilingual education in their curriculum.

Culturally Relevant Teaching

In addition to bilingual education, scholars have discussed the role of culturally relevant pedagogy in facilitating the success of racial and ethnic minority students in mathematics and science in K–12 education (Ladson-Billings, 1995b; Lipman, 1995). Ladson-Billings asserted that culturally relevant pedagogical practices must meet three criteria: they must focus on (1) developing students academically, (2) nurturing and supporting students' cultural competence, and (3) developing students' critical competence. Lipman conducted an ethnographic study of three Black teachers and provided a concrete example of culturally relevant pedagogy for Black students. More specifically, the teachers held high expectations for all students and instilled in them that they all had the desire and potential to learn. They also established meaningful commitments and relationships with students' families to help facilitate the students' academic achievement. In addition, the teachers validated the students' non-Eurocentric lives. Finally, they celebrated the richness of the students' language, culture, and experience.

Culturally relevant pedagogy is an important consideration because, when science and math teachers instruct from a Eurocentric point of view, they fail to include an approach that connects curriculum, instruction, and assessment to the experiences, cultures, and traditions of racial and ethnic minority students (Anderson, 1990; Tate, 1994). Such Eurocentric pedagogy, imposing racial inferiority on racial and ethnic minority students, causes those students to view mathematics as a subject that is exclusively for White males and hinders those students' ability to see the applicability of science and mathematics to their own lives. Thus, it is important to consider the role of culturally relevant pedagogy in efforts to serve minority students.

Research illustrates that incorporating culturally relevant pedagogy into science and mathematics instruction has a positive impact on Black students (Denson, Avery, and Schell, 2010; Ladson-Billings, 1995a; Lipman, 1995; Shujaa, 1995; Tate, 1994, 1995a). Denson and colleagues, for example, conducted an in-depth qualitative study of seven Black high school students regarding their perception of engineering and found that using culturally relevant pedagogy in K–12 was important to attracting those students to engineering programs. In addition, Tate (1995a) provided further evidence of the utility of incorporating culturally relevant pedagogy into mathematics instruction by explaining how one teacher had a positive impact on students' interest and success in mathematics by including social issues that Blacks often encounter in education and society into her pedagogical practices.

In addition to the research on the impact of culturally relevant pedagogy on Black students, several scholars have discussed the importance of incorporating culturally specific knowledge into pedagogical practices when teaching other racial and ethnic minority students as well (Barnhardt and Kawagley, 2005; Gutstein, Lipman, Hernandez, and de los Reyes, 1997; Kaomea, 2003; Nelson-Barber and Estrin, 1995; Rendón and Triana, 1989; Rolon, 2003; Sheets, 1995). Nelson-Barber and Estrin, for instance, explain that teachers need to be intentional about using culturally relevant pedagogy when teaching mathematics and science to Native Americans. They suggest that incorporating the unique aspects of Native Americans' culture will increase their rate of academic success in mathematics and science. Rolon argued that adopting culturally sensitive pedagogy into classroom instruction is necessary to enhance the educational efficacy of Hispanic students. In addition, as we discuss in the next chapter, Kiang (1997, 2002) demonstrated that such culturally relevant pedagogy can have a profound positive impact on the experiences and outcomes of Southeast Asian American students. Therefore, although culturally relevant pedagogical practices in K–12 science and mathematics are lacking, the incorporation of such practices could have a positive influence on racial and ethnic minority students' success in the STEM education circuit.

Early Exposure to Careers in STEM

Research also indicates that a relationship exists between early exposure to science and mathematics careers and long-term success in the STEM circuit (Anderson, 1990; Fries-Britt, Younger, and Hall, 2010; Fullilove and Treisman, 1990; Oakes, 1990; Powell, 1990; Seymour and Hewitt, 1997). Indeed, it has been suggested that, when racial and ethnic minority students have greater access to information about careers in STEM and quality career guidance, they are more inclined to develop interests in mathematics and science fields (Seymour and Hewitt, 1997). Thus, such access and guidance might be critical in fostering minority students' interest in STEM.

One way that racial and ethnic minority students can be exposed to STEM careers early is through connecting with role models in those professions (Lewis, 2003; Tornatzky, Macias, and Solis, 2006). Access and exposure to role models is important because visualizing or seeing people who achieve positive outcomes (such as attaining a professional position in the STEM workforce) can raise one's self-efficacy, the belief that he or she too can achieve those outcomes (Bandura, 1977). Several people in the STEM fields have asserted that the availability of role models could be one factor that facilitates the success of minority students in the STEM circuit (see, for example, American Association for the Advancement of Science, 1989).

Although researchers have provided evidence of the significant impact that teachers and counselors can have on minority students' success in STEM (Bissell, 2000; Brown, 2002; Clewell, Anderson, and Thorpe, 1992; Moore, 2006), evidence that highlights the impact of minority role models—that is, individuals who model minority success in STEM professions—is difficult to find. Research does suggest that having parents who are STEM professionals is correlated with success in STEM education (Astin and Astin, 1992; Grandy, 1994), but the actual effects of nonparental role models are uncertain. In addition, although evidence indicates that peers can also function as powerful role models (Murphey, 1995, l996), the influence of peer role models is also a relatively unexplored area of inquiry. In an earlier study, Thompson and Lewis (2005) explained that empirical support for the relationship between role models and student achievement in mathematics is lacking, and our review of literature is consistent with this assessment. We believe this is a critical area for future research in STEM education.

Interest in STEM Subjects

In addition to the connection between early exposure to STEM fields and success in the STEM circuit, research shows that a relationship exists between racial and ethnic minority students' having an interest in mathematics and science in K–12 and their persistence and success in the STEM circuit (Astin and Astin, 1992; Bonous-Hammarth, 2000; Hall and Post-Kammer, 1987; Hilton, Hsia, Solórzano, and Benton, 1989; Hrabowski and Maton, 1995; Oakes, 1990). For example, Hall and Post-Kammer reported that early interest in science is positively related to students' desire to major in science in college. Similarly, Hrabowski and Maton noted that interest in science is one predictor of future academic success in the physical sciences. Furthermore, Moore's qualitative study (2006) of forty-two Black engineering students who attended a PWI found that having a passion for engineering and mathematics in primary and secondary school contributed to their persistence in higher education.

But it should also be noted that, although interest in STEM majors or careers is an important precursor to the success of racial and ethnic minorities in the STEM circuit, a lack of interest in those careers does not appear to be the primary source of the high departure rates of minority students from STEM education (Anderson and Kim, 2006; Cullinane and Leegwater, 2009; Dowd, Malcom, and Bensimon, 2009; Elliott and others, 1996). For example, it has been reported that one-third of first-year Black, Hispanic, and Native American students and 43 percent of their AAPI peers intend to major in science and engineering (May and Chubin, 2003).

Self-Efficacy in STEM

Another conclusion that can be drawn from existing research is that racial and ethnic minority students' self-efficacy in STEM—that is, their confidence in their ability to learn math and science in primary and secondary education—is a salient predictor of success in STEM education (Colbeck, Cabrera, and Terenzini, 2001; Perna and others, 2009). For instance, using data from the 1971 and 1980 Cooperative Institutional Research Program, which contains a wealth of information from students' precollege years, undergraduate and graduate education, and postsecondary employment, Leslie, McClure, and Oaxaca (1998) found that self-efficacy is an important predictor of success in STEM for racial and ethnic minority students. In addition, using the nationally representative NELS (88:00) data, Holt (2006) noted a relationship between racial and ethnic minority high school students' confidence in their ability to do well in mathematics and enrollment in higher-level mathematics courses. Holt further explained that students' confidence in their ability to do well in mathematics was a predictor of persistence in the STEM education circuit.

The impact of racial and ethnic minority students' self-efficacy on their success in STEM is complicated when considering it simultaneously with other factors. According to Seymour and Hewitt (1997), Blacks and Hispanics experience a conflict between overconfidence and poor preparation, which impairs their success in the STEM circuit. More specifically, many racial and ethnic minority students who major in STEM in college come from high schools where they were viewed as academically superior compared with their peers. In these schools, they developed strong confidence but lacked advanced skills that are necessary to achieve their aspirations because of their lack of participation in Advanced Placement classes. As a result, when those students entered college, they were overwhelmed and at greater risk of switching to less intense majors or dropping out of college.

In summary, a number of factors in K–12 education are instrumental in helping facilitate the success of racial and ethnic minority students in STEM. Being aware of these factors could play a critical role in helping educators, researchers, and policymakers enhance success for racial and ethnic minority students in the STEM circuit. The next section of this chapter delineates initiatives in K–12 to enhance the preparedness and success of racial and ethnic minority students in the STEM circuit.

K–12 Initiatives That Contribute to Preparedness and Success Among Minority Students in STEM

A small body of research highlights programs in K–12 that help facilitate the long-term success of racial and ethnic minority students in the STEM circuit. We review this literature in hopes that these programs will provide practitioners with concrete examples of how some educators have created supportive structures that may increase success among racial and ethnic minority students in the STEM education circuit. We focus on three programs: the Preengineering Program at the University of Akron, the Detroit Area Pre-College Engineering Program, and Say YES to a Youngster's Future. We focus on these programs because, unlike most, empirical evidence of these programs' efficacy was available. We also caution readers, however, that the researchers who have examined these programs have often failed to report on the rigor of their methods or pay attention to the aspects of these programs that are ineffective. Thus, the findings reported in this section should be interpreted with caution.

Preengineering Program at the University of Akron

The University of Akron has promulgated an initiative to increase the enrollment and success of first-generation college students (that is, neither parent earned a bachelor's degree) and Blacks, Hispanics, Native Americans, and AAPIs in the STEM circuit (Lam and others, 2005). More specifically, the university has established a summer and after-school preengineering program, which has several goals:

Reinforcing the self-confidence of racial and ethnic minority high school students in the STEM circuit;

Enhancing students' problem-solving abilities;

Increasing students' awareness of careers in STEM;

Using diagnostic testing to identify deficiencies; and

Providing students with opportunities to use computers and become familiar with the use of word processing, spreadsheets, mathematics software, and the Internet.

Approximately forty students in grades 9 through 12 are admitted into the Preengineering Program each year. Participants must meet the following criteria:

Live in Ohio, Pennsylvania, Indiana, or Michigan;

Demonstrate interest or potential in Advanced Placement courses in mathematics or science;

Demonstrate a level of maturity and independence to enable them to live away from home for six weeks;

Meet federal poverty guidelines;

Achieve a grade point average of 2.5;

Attend a conference with parents; and

Engage in an interview with the director of the program.

Students or their families are not financially responsible for participating in the program. The U.S. Department of Education covers all necessary expenses for students. Students who are formally admitted to the program receive a weekly stipend during the summer and a monthly stipend during the year.

For six weeks during the summer, selected students participate in a series of academic classes such as English, mathematics, physics, biology, and a foreign language. Simultaneously, program participants interact with engineering faculty and staff for about an hour and thirty minutes daily. In this summer program, participants work collaboratively with faculty and staff on building projects, laboratory demonstrations, and other structured learning activities. Faculty members also provide students with advice on career planning and mentoring. In addition to collaborative experiences with faculty, students work collectively with each other on projects that include tasks such as designing bridges, building model roller coasters, designing rockets, testing building materials, and designing electronic circuits.

Aside from the summer program, students also participate in a series of career workshops at regional manufacturing companies and research facilities and attend weekly tutoring sessions throughout the school year. These workshops help students become better exposed to careers in the STEM profession.

Furthermore, they provide an opportunity for students to have one-on-one discussions with the engineers. For participants who are out of state, the Internet serves as a conduit through which they can participate. Tutoring occurs in partnership with the College of Engineering at the University of Akron. More specifically, engineering students from the Increasing Diversity in Engineering Academics program and student members of the National Society of Black Engineers volunteer six hours per week and provide mentorship for participants of the preengineering program.

Lam and others (2005) argue that the preengineering program has been tremendously successful. More specifically, they conducted descriptive analyses of data from 1994 through 2004 and found that 100 percent of the program's participants graduated from high school and 94 percent of those students entered college. The authors concluded that "the University of Akron summer integrated and year-round academic programs have increased access and retention of identifiable under-represented students pursuing STEM careers. . . . The pre-engineering curricula actually results in several significant student outcomes such as (1) increase[d] grade point average, (2) less anxiety toward math and science, (3) fostering the can-do attitude, and (4) increasing personal self-esteem" (p. 18). These findings are limited, however, because sufficient details about the methods used to assess the program were not reported and it is therefore difficult to draw definitive conclusions about the effectiveness of the initiative. Moreover, the long-term effects of this program have not been examined.

Detroit Area Pre-College Engineering Program

Another K–12 program that focuses on increasing the enrollment and success of Black, Hispanic, and Native American students in the STEM circuit is the Detroit Area Pre-College Engineering Program (DAPCEP) (Hill, 1990). Implemented with a grant from the Alfred P. Sloan Foundation in 1976, the DAPCEP works in concert with the Detroit Public School System, local universities, major corporations, and businesses to increase the number of middle and high school students interested in pursuing STEM careers in Detroit.

The DAPCEP provides instructional and motivational activities throughout the school year as well as during the summer for racial and ethnic minority students in grades 7 through 12. More specifically, the DAPCEP includes three interrelated components:

The summer skill intensification program, which offers classes in mathematics, science, computer science, and communication in grades 9 through 12;

Saturday enrichment classes, which are held at several area universities and consist of courses in physics, chemistry, laboratory skills, science, technical writing, chemical, civil, electrical, and mechanical engineering, algebra, trigonometry, calculus, and computer science; and

Preengineering classes in science and engineering that are held at public schools in Detroit. Students participate in science fairs, attend field trips, view presentations by technical speakers, research minority engineers and scientists, and participate in research symposiums.

To be accepted into the DAPCEP, students need to have an interest in mathematics and science, have a minimum grade point average of at least a C+, and have a recommendation from a teacher or counselor.

Although no recent data exist on the efficacy of the DAPCEP, in 1990, Hill sent a survey to 3,170 students who participated in the program from 1976 until 1986. Of that number, 584 people returned the survey. The results revealed that 74 percent of DAPCEP alumni who were enrolled in college were majoring in a STEM-related field and an impressive 81 percent of DAPCEP alumni who were college graduates attained a degree in STEM. These statistics, however, are descriptive in nature and do not clarify whether the program had a causal effect on outcomes in STEM.

Say YES to a Youngster's Future

Another program that was implemented to increase the interest and academic success of Blacks and Hispanics in STEM education is Say Yes to a Youngster's Future (Beane, 1990). This program emerged in 1987 with financial support from the Shell Company Foundation and the National Urban Coalition's Schools Project. The Say Yes program has several goals:

Improving the confidence and competencies of teachers in mathematics and science;

Increasing the mathematics and science competencies and interests of minority elementary school students;

Facilitating the involvement of parents and communities in mathematics and science education; and

Increasing the skill level of racial and ethnic minority students in mathematics and science so they will be prepared for advanced mathematics and science work beyond secondary school (Beane, 1990).

The Say Yes program initially started as a two-year pilot program in the District of Columbia but has since been implemented in schools in Houston and New Orleans. Several criteria determine whether schools can participate: enrollment must be at least 75 percent Black and Hispanic, enrollment must include underachieving students based on their scores on standardized tests in mathematics and science, and the school's principal and a team of teachers must be strongly committed to the program. The Say Yes program comprises four critical elements:

School-based teams: Such teams comprise a small group of teachers and the principal. The teams are charged with participating in staff development activities as well as planning and implementing the project at the school.

Staff development: Using test scores and classroom observations, the school district mathematics and science coordinators work closely with the school-based team to identify areas in the elementary school curriculum that need improvement. School-based teams participate in summer programs and in in-service programs during the school year, where they are trained by master secondary teachers in science and mathematics to develop greater competency with the areas in the curriculum identified as weak. Additional training includes Say Yes Family Math, which helps provide the school team with appropriate philosophy and structure for involving parents in informal school-focused mathematics activities.

Saturday family math and science: Although the times that sessions are offered vary across school districts, they are typically held once a month during the school year. Some sessions are held at the school and others take place at community-based facilities such as zoos, museums, and nature centers and last from two to three hours. Topics include explorations of electricity, chemistry, simple machines, light, weather, flight, fossils, insects, animal behavior, plants, and astronomy. Families work in concert with teachers and students, using activity sheets and instructional material. Spanish translations of the instructional forms are provided for Hispanic families with limited English proficiency. Families also leave the session with activities to try at home with the proper instructional materials needed to do so.

Outreach: To build community support for science and mathematics education, the Say Yes program employs a variety of approaches (for example, conferences, active distribution of information about the Saturday family math and science program, and T-shirts). Efforts to build community support and raise awareness include the schools, representatives from the business sector, political leaders, parents, and community-based organizations.

Research indicates that the Say Yes program has had a positive impact on students' academic performance in mathematics and science (Beane, 1990). More specifically, data from students who took the Metropolitan Achievement Test (MAT) in spring 1987 as a pretest and spring 1988 as a posttest, with classrooms of teachers participating in Say Yes and those who did not compared and students participating in the Saturday Program and those who did not compared, revealed the following results:

The students of teachers participating in Say Yes gained 28.95 points in mathematics, which is equivalent to a 1.2-grade increase among participants, compared with an 18.56-point gain among students in the control classrooms (Beane, 1990).

In reading, the students of teachers participating in Say Yes gained 28.52 points (a 0.7-grade equivalent), while students in the control classrooms gained 15.97 points (a 0.4-grade equivalent). Furthermore, students participating in the Saturday Math Program scored higher on the MAT test in mathematics and reading compared with the control group. Specifically, participants gained 25.97 points in mathematics on the MAT, whereas nonparticipants gained 15.65 points, equivalent to a 1.1-grade increase for participants versus a 0.7-grade increase for nonparticipants. Participating students also gained 25.00 points (a 0.5-grade equivalent gain) in reading on the MAT, while nonparticipants gained 12.24 points (a 0.4-grade equivalent gain) (Beane, 1990).

It is unclear whether the evaluators of this program used an experimental or quasi-experimental design in conducting their analyses. Although this evidence supports the efficacy of three programs, this literature is sparse and much remains to be learned about whether such STEM initiatives in K 12 education positively affect minority student outcomes in the STEM circuit.

In sum, existing evidence indicates that STEM-specific programs in K–12 can positively affect racial and ethnic minority student outcomes in STEM. That evidence is not strong, however, and definitive conclusions about the impact of precollege STEM-specific initiatives on minority students' success in STEM should await more inferential studies that can support causal connections. Moreover, extant literature does not critically analyze and identify the extent to which various components of STEM-specific precollege programs influence the outcomes of racial and ethnic minority students, either positively or negatively.

Conclusion

In sum, empirical research demonstrates a relationship between academic preparedness in K–12 and success in the STEM circuit. Notwithstanding, racial and ethnic minority students are least likely to be academically prepared in K–12 to be successful in the STEM circuit. This chapter identified factors in K–12 that contribute to the lack of academic preparedness among racial and ethnic minority students. Furthermore, it delineated factors in K–12 that facilitate the success of racial and ethnic minority students in the STEM circuit. And it focused on initiatives in K–12 to enhance the success of racial and ethnic minority students in the STEM education circuit.

This chapter illustrates the critical relationship between preparedness in K–12 and success in the STEM circuit and indicates that many racial and ethnic minority students are not adequately prepared in K–12 to be successful in the STEM circuit. Thus stronger emphasis must be placed on effectively preparing minority students in K–12 to be successful in the STEM circuit. One way to improve the success of these students is identifying ways to effectively deal with factors that contribute to their lack of academic preparedness in K–12, which are inextricably linked to their ability to succeed in the STEM circuit. Focusing on the success factors and expanding STEM programs identified in this chapter provide useful ways to constructively increase the preparedness and success of minority students in STEM.

Factors That Influence Success Among Racial and Ethnic Minority College Students in the STEM Circuit

T HE PREVIOUS CHAPTER REVIEWED literature on factors encountered by racial and ethnic minority students in K–12 education that influence their preparedness, or lack thereof, and success in the STEM circuit. This chapter focuses on factors that have been associated with different levels of success among minority students in STEM after they enter college: (1) colorblind meritocracy and affirmative action, (2) economic factors, (3) institutional type, (4) campus environments, (5) interactions with institutional agents, (6) psychological factors, and (7) STEM-specific opportunity and support programs. The following sections discuss research that examines the impact of these factors on racial and ethnic minority students in STEM in higher education. Because much of the research on racial and ethnic minority students' success is based on theories that provide useful frameworks for understanding these influences on success, this chapter introduces important theoretical frameworks at the beginning of each section. For comprehensiveness, the following sections consider research on both racial and ethnic minority college students in general and in STEM fields specifically.

The Role of Colorblind Meritocracy and Affirmative Action

The concept of meritocracy first appeared in Young's *The Rise of the Meritocracy* (1958). Today, the concept of meritocracy—the idea that, if people work hard enough, nothing can stop them from achieving their dreams—is a value endorsed by the majority of American society (McNamee and Miller, 2009).

Moreover, many believers in meritocracy argue that people are rewarded for their hard work and achievements, regardless of their racial background, implying that the nation's meritocracy is colorblind in nature.

Although many espouse the belief of a colorblind meritocracy, one major problem with meritocratic perspectives, of course, is that racism has always been or continues to be embedded in the social fabric of the American society (Haney and Hurtado, 1994; Harper, Patton, and Wooden, 2009). Indeed, evidence reviewed in the previous chapter highlights how systemic factors such as social disparities in funding schools disadvantage minorities. Thus what many purport to be a colorblind system of hard work and proportional economic and social rewards can also be considered a system in which racism—and other forms of oppression—functions to redistribute resources to groups that already possess them (for example, affluent White populations).

In many ways, standardized tests are a linchpin of meritocracy in education. Standardized tests are designed to assess the investment of students' hard work and academic abilities, and they are used to decide who is rewarded with rites of passage to institutions of higher education. Scholars, however, have also attacked standardized tests because research shows that standardized testing is culturally biased toward racial and ethnic minorities because their content is Eurocentric (Bennett, McWhorter, and Kuykendall, 2006; Fleming, 2000, 2002; Grant, 2004; Jencks and Phillips, 1998), and they lack power to predict academic success (Fleming and Garcia, 1998). Consequently, several colleges have elected to stop using standardized testing in admission decisions (JBHE Foundation, 2005–06).

One highly contentious phenomenon aimed at combating the racial inequities engendered by racism and perpetuated by supposedly colorblind meritocratic systems is affirmative action. Established under President Lyndon B. Johnson, affirmative action aims to promote access and equity for minorities in programs receiving federal funds (Brown, 1999). Many racial and ethnic minorities have benefited enormously from these policies in respect to higher education. Educational institutions have used affirmative action to provide access and increase the number of minorities in higher education. Since its implementation, the constitutionality of this policy has been challenged vigorously in the Supreme Court.

Over the past three decades, the Supreme Court has consistently upheld the constitutionality of affirmative action. In *University of California Regents* v. *Bakke* [438 U.S. 265 (1978)], the Court ruled five to four that considering race in admission is permissible as long as the program is "precisely tailored and serves a compelling governmental interest" but prohibited the use of racial quotas. Almost two decades later, in *Hopwood* v. *Texas* [78 F.3d 932 (5th Circuit, 1996)], the U.S. Court of Appeals ruled that the University of Texas Law School in 1996 could not use race-sensitive policies. Around that time, California voters passed Proposition 209, which prohibited affirmative action in public entities throughout the state (Pusser, 2001). Other states, including Washington and Florida, have also prohibited the use of race-conscious policies. Although California, Florida, and Texas have implemented alternative plans to supplant the efficacy of race-sensitive policies, they have not been nearly as effective in promoting access for minorities (Horn and Flores, 2003).

In *Grutter* v. *Bollinger* [539 U.S. 306 (2003)], the Supreme Court reaffirmed educational institutions' ability to use race to attain a diverse student body as long as it is narrowly tailored and does not function as a quota system but cautioned that race-sensitive policies should be temporary: "We are mindful, however, that a core purpose of the Fourteenth Amendment was to do away with all government imposed discrimination based on race. . . . Accordingly, race conscious admission policies must be limited in time. This requirement reflects that racial classifications, however compelling their goals, are potentially so dangerous that they may be employed no more than the interest demands. . . . We see no reason to exempt race conscious admissions programs from the requirement that all government use of race must have a logical end point" (p. 342).

Notwithstanding the Court's ruling on affirmative action, Schmidt (2006) and Glater (2006) have argued that attacks on affirmative action prompt universities to abandon race-sensitive policies. According to Fleming (2000), the dismantlement of affirmative action may prompt a greater reliance on standardized tests such as SAT scores. Efforts to dismantle affirmative action in higher education protect an allegedly colorblind meritocratic system and its oppression of racial and ethnic minority students in those structures and therefore function as an impediment of those individuals' progress through the STEM circuit.

The Impact of Economic Influences

Economic influences have been identified as an important predictor of success among minority college students in STEM. Human Capital Theory (Becker, 1964) suggests that college students make choices based on the perceived costs and benefits of various options. This theory implies that, the more college students believe that continuing their path down the STEM circuit is economically beneficial, the greater the likelihood that they will choose to persist in those fields. Accordingly, a plethora of research has shed light on the role of financial factors in success among racial and ethnic minority college students in general and the success of racial and ethnic minority students in STEM specifically (see, for example, Adelman, 2006; Arbona and Novy, 1990; Branch-Brioso, 2009; Cabrera, Nora, and Castañada, 1992; Cabrera, Stampen, and Hansen, 1990; Cofer, 2000; Cofer and Somers, 2000; Cullinane and Leegwater, 2009; DesJardins, Ahlburg, and McCall, 2002; Dowd and Coury, 2006; Heller, 2003; Millett, 2003; Museus, 2010b; Paulsen and St. John, 1997, 2002; St. John, 1991, 2003). This evidence suggests that ability to pay for college, financial aid, and hours working influence minority students' success in STEM.

The Role of Ability to Pay for College

The success of racial and ethnic minority college students in STEM is in part a consequence of their ability to pay for college (see, for example, Adelman, 2006; Arbona and Novy, 1990; Astin, 1982, 1993; Branch-Brioso, 2009; Cullinane and Leegwater, 2009; Green and Glasson, 2009; Hernandez, 2000; Hernandez and Lopez, 2004–05; James, 2000; Kane, Beals, Valeau, and Johnson, 2004; Maton, Hrabowski, and Schmitt, 2000). Indeed, several studies have found that financial factors are one of the most important predictors of decisions to leave college among racial and ethnic minority students in STEM (Hurtado and others, 2007; Maton and Hrabrowski, 2004; May and Chubin, 2003; Perna and others, 2009; Seymour and Hewitt, 1997). Seymour and Hewitt, for example, conducted a three-year ethnographic study that included individual interviews and focus groups with more than 460 minority students and concluded that insufficient financial resources was one of the most salient reasons that their attrition in STEM fields was higher than among Whites. Seymour and Hewitt's finding are not surprising, given that Black, Hispanic, Native American, and Southeast Asian American students are more likely to come from economically disadvantaged backgrounds than their White peers (Gándara, 2006; Garrison, 1987; Green and Glasson, 2009; Museus, 2009, forthcoming; Museus and Kiang, 2009).

Several trends underscore the importance of considering ability to pay in understanding the success of racial and ethnic minority students in STEM. First, given continuously rising tuition rates and increased reliance on loans in the composition of financial aid packages (Museus, 2010b), it is unlikely that threats to racial and ethnic minority college students' ability to pay will subside. Second, evidence suggests that students in STEM are more likely to be awarded scholarships based on merit than need (Fenske, Porter, and DuBrock, 2000). Because minority students are more likely to be inadequately prepared for STEM majors, the allocation of resources to fund merit-based rather than need-based aid can also adversely affect their ability to pay. The following sections discuss three financial factors that affect ability to pay among minority students in STEM: college cost, financial aid, and employment.

The Impact of College Cost

College costs have been rising significantly for the past two decades (Choy, 2004). Currently, annual tuition and fees for a public four-year institution are $7,020 for in-state students and $11,528 for out-of-state students, but that number is $26,273 for those attending private four-year campuses (College Board, 2010). Moreover, because college costs are rising faster than average family income, an increasing number of students have unmet financial need and greater difficulties paying for college (Breland and others, 2002; Choy, 1999). Two primary ways that racial and ethnic minority students in STEM cope with the rising costs of college are by using financial aid awards and working.

The Role of Financial Aid

Evidence suggests that financial aid influences success among racial and ethnic minorities in STEM, but this relationship is complex, with some types of financial aid having a positive influence and others having a questionable impact. Financial aid awards in general are positively correlated with success among racial and ethnic minority students in engineering (Georges, 1999; U.S. Department of Education, 2000). Specifically, gifts in the form of scholarships and grants have been linked to higher rates of persistence and degree attainment for minority students (General Accounting Office, 1995; St. John, 2002; Swail, Redd, and Perna, 2003). One analysis, for example, revealed that an additional $1,000 in grants lowered the probability of Black and Hispanic students leaving college by 7 to 8 percent (GAO, 1995). Given that low-income students in STEM are less likely to complete college degrees (Fenske, Porter, and DuBrock, 2000), access to financial aid, and especially grants, is particularly important for these undergraduates.

The influence of loans appears to be more complex, with researchers finding loan amounts to be both positively and negatively correlated with success (for discussion, see Museus, 2010b). Although more research is needed to make sense of these conflicting results, what is evident is that loans appear to promote success among White students more effectively than among racial and ethnic minorities (General Accounting Office, 1995), which could be because minority students are more sensitive to college costs and more averse to taking out loans to finance their college education (Ehrenberg, 1991; Kaltenbaugh, St. John, and Starkey, 1999). Regardless of the reason for the differential effects of loans on attaining a college degree, the fact that loans might not be as likely to increase success among minority students in STEM is important, given that policymakers have increasingly relied on loans in the composition of financial aid packages (Museus, 2010b; St. John, 2003; Wei and Carroll, 2004).

It has also been noted that much of the influence of financial aid on persistence and attainment might be indirect (DesJardins, Ahlburg, and McCall, 2002; Pascarella and Terenzini, 1991, 2005; Paulsen and St. John, 1997; St. John, Cabrera, Nora, and Asker, 2000; St. John, Paulsen, and Starkey, 1996). For example, financial aid awards for students who need them can remove financial barriers to students' engagement in academic and social activities and subsequently contribute to persistence and completion (St. John, Cabrera, Nora, and Asker, 2000). It is reasonable then to hypothesize that financial aid can indirectly influence racial and ethnic minority students' success in STEM by eliminating the need to work long hours as well.

The Impact of Employment

Evidence suggests that employment influences success among racial and ethnic minority students in STEM but that impact depends on the location and nature of work. Extant research on the general college student population suggests that working off campus is negatively associated with success—especially working more than twenty-five hours per week off campus (Pascarella and others, 1998). Alternatively, existing empirical evidence appears to suggest that working on campus can positively influence success (Institute for Higher Education Policy, 2001; Kuh and others, 2007). Although the causes of the conflicting influence of working on and off campus are not clear, it is possible that on-campus work enhances students' connections to their institution, while off-campus work hinders them (Astin, 1993; Pascarella and Terenzini, 1991). Finally, some indications suggest that working on a research project with professors is positively associated with success among underrepresented minorities in STEM (Hurtado and others, 2007), but by and large the impact of specific kinds of work on success has not been the focus of empirical inquiry.

Inability to pay for college or insufficient financial resources, however, can force racial and ethnic minority students in STEM (as well as other majors) to work a substantial number of hours to pay for their expenses, thereby adversely affecting the likelihood of their success. Indeed, researchers have revealed that, because of inadequate finances, many minority students in general and in STEM in particular need to have a job to compensate for their school and living expenses (see, for example, Arbona, and Novy, 1990; Branch-Brioso, 2009; Green and Glasson, 2009; Hernandez, 2000; Hernandez and Lopez, 2004–05; James, 2000; Varma, 2009). The pressure to work to compensate for financial struggles can disproportionately hinder success among racial and ethnic minority students. For example, Hispanics who encounter financial concerns often find jobs that hinder their academic performance in mathematics and science courses (Arbona and Novy, 1990; Hernandez, 2000; Hernandez and Lopez, 2004–05; Padilla, Trevino, Gonzalez, and Trevino, 1997). In addition, Hispanic students are more likely than other racial groups to work longer hours, which has been associated with their leaving college (Sedlacek, Longerbeam, and Alatorre, 2003). Nevertheless, it is likely that low-income

AAPI, Black, and Native American students in STEM are also likely to work long hours and suffer negative consequences on their success.

In sum, the ability to pay for college is a major factor influencing the success of racial and ethnic minority students in STEM. Rising college costs, trends toward increased reliance on loans in the composition of financial aid packages, and the emphasis on merit-based aid in STEM fields might all contribute to financial pressures for minority students. Although those undergraduates can work to compensate for inadequate finances, working too many hours can also hinder their success. It is important to note that most of the research on financial influences on the success of racial and ethnic minority students in STEM has been focused on Black and Hispanic students. Much remains to be learned about how economic factors influence the success of Native American or Southeast Asian American students. Moreover, existing literature that is specifically focused on STEM tends to examine how economic factors such as work hinder success. Questions remain about whether certain types of employment such as off-campus jobs in the STEM fields have a greater impact on progress through the STEM circuit than non-STEM jobs. Although the discussion in the previous chapter that highlights the potential impact that being exposed to STEM fields can have on progress in the STEM circuit might suggest that racial and ethnic minority students who have jobs in STEM-related fields are more likely to succeed in the STEM circuit, future research is needed to test this assumption.

The Impact of Minority-Serving Institutions and Selective Institutions

Research suggests that two institutional characteristics may influence the success of racial and ethnic minority students in STEM. First, it indicates that campuses classified as minority-serving institutions (MSIs) might have a positive effect on success among minority students in STEM (Fries-Britt, Younger, and Hall, 2010; Kim and Conrad, 2006; Lent and others, 2005; National Science Board, 2004; Palmer, Davis, and Thompson, 2010; Solórzano, 1995; Suitts, 2003; Wenglinsky, 1997). Second, existing empirical evidence suggests that highly selective institutions may be less effective at graduating minority college students in STEM fields (Bonous-Hammarth, 2006; Chang, Cerna, Han, and Sàenz, 2008).

MSIs produce a large proportion of the nation's racial and ethnic minority college graduates in STEM (National Science Board, 2004). Indeed, seventeen of the top twenty leading producers of Black bachelor's degree recipients in general are historically Black colleges and universities (HBCUs) (Borden and Brown, 2004). In the area of STEM specifically, HBCUs account for only approximately 3 percent of all four-year institutions, but they confer 26 to 31 percent of baccalaureate degrees in science and engineering annually (Babco, 2003). In fact, research clearly and consistently indicates that HBCUs are relatively effective at producing minority graduates in STEM fields (Kim and Conrad, 2006; Lent and others, 2005; Solórzano, 1995; Suitts, 2003; Wenglinsky, 1997). The effectiveness of HBCUs at producing minority graduates in STEM could be the result of many factors. For example, research suggests that the extent to which a student's racial background is represented on campus might be correlated with the validation of his or her racial and ethnic backgrounds and, subsequently, success (Museus, Jayakumar, and Robinson, forthcoming), although this relationship has not specifically been examined among STEM students. Furthermore, as a result of the large representation of Black students at HBCUs, those undergraduates are likely to encounter relatively positive environments compared with their counterparts at PWIs (Allen, 1992; Anderson, 1990; Lent and others, 2005; Palmer, 2010b; Palmer and Gasman, 2008). Lent and others, for example, conducted a survey of 487 engineering students across three institutions and found that students at the two HBCUs reported higher rates of support compared with their peers at the PWIs. Research on the extent to which it is the supportive nature of the environment or other institutional factors that primarily account for the large number of Black college graduates in STEM at HBCUs, however, precludes any definitive conclusions.

Although research is lacking in examinations that statistically link specific aspects of the environment at HBCUs to positive educational outcomes, a few inquiries describe some institutional factors that might be responsible for HBCUs' effectiveness at producing large numbers of racial and ethnic minority STEM graduates. In a qualitative case study of one HBCU, for example,

Perna and others (2009) found several factors that facilitate success among students in STEM at that institution, including supportive environments, smaller class sizes, accessibility of faculty offices, faculty encouragement and support, and a wide range of available academic support services, tutoring services, and peer support. Similarly, Fries-Britt, Younger, and Hall (2010) interviewed 110 racial and ethnic minority students in STEM and reported that some faculty members at HBCUs go out of their way to teach and work directly with students, spend time with students outside the classroom, and even invite students into their homes and allow them to spend time with their families. Given that many of these realities are lacking in or completely absent from the experiences of minority undergraduates in STEM at PWIs, they shed some light on how HBCUs can be successful at producing large numbers of STEM graduates.

Like HBCUs, Hispanic-serving institutions (HSIs) play a critical role in the education of Hispanic students (Contreras, Bensimon, and Malcom, 2008). Although HSIs represent 8 percent of all postsecondary institutions, half of all Hispanic undergraduates are enrolled at these institutions (Dowd, Malcom, and Bensimon, 2009). Moreover, because HSIs enroll a disproportionate number of Hispanic students, they award a disproportionate number of STEM degrees to Hispanics as well (Dowd, Malcom, and Bensimon, 2009). Given that research on Hispanic students' experiences at HSIs has not kept pace with the rate at which the population is growing, it is unclear whether HSIs affect Hispanic undergraduates in the same ways that HBCUs affect Black college students.

Nevertheless, because of the large population of Hispanics that they serve, HSIs are uniquely positioned to act as an important gateway to the STEM circuit for Hispanic students (Dowd, Malcom, and Bensimon, 2009). In fact, Congress recently recognized HSIs for their contribution in increasing STEM achievement among Hispanics. Furthermore in 2009, the America COMPETES Act—a federal act aimed at responding to concerns about America's competitiveness in the global marketplace and increasing the nation's investments in science and engineering research—permitted the NSF to create programs aimed at helping HSIs improve STEM education. This initiative is expected to improve STEM education at HSIs and to increase retention and degree attainment for Hispanics pursing degrees in STEM education. According to Lederman (2010), one interesting outcome of this initiative has been that researchers at the University of Southern California's Center for Urban Education have proposed a set of metrics that institutions can use to gauge their progress in getting more Hispanics interested in the STEM circuit and ultimately earning STEM degrees.

Although evidence demonstrates the efficacy of MSIs in producing success for racial and ethnic minority students in STEM, the extent to which these factors statistically explain the success of MSIs at producing STEM graduates is unclear. In a recent study, Hurtado and others (2007) provide evidence that the relationship between MSI status and minority students' success in STEM might be confounded by the lower selectivity of those institutions. They examined a national sample using linear regression techniques and concluded that attendance at an MSI was positively and significantly correlated with Black, Hispanic, and Native American students' academic adjustment. When institutional selectivity was added to the equation, however, the influence of attending an MSI disappeared, suggesting that the effects of attending an MSI and the influence of institutional selectivity on academic adjustment interact with one another.

Indeed, although evidence indicates that attending highly selective institutions positively contributes to success among the general college student population (Bowen and Bok, 1998; Kane, 1998), research also indicates that institutional selectivity negatively affects the success of racial and ethnic minority students in STEM fields specifically (Bonous-Hammarth, 2000; Chang, Cerna, Han, and Sàenz, 2008; Smyth and McArdle, 2004). Elliott and others (1996), for example, found drastic differences between the graduation rates of White (61 percent) and racial and ethnic minority (34 percent) students in STEM at four elite PWIs and concluded that affirmative action admissions policies that permit unprepared racial and ethnic minority college students in STEM to attend selective institutions contribute to the lower rates of success among that population.

Some researchers have argued that this relationship is a result of a "mismatch" between highly selective institutions and minority undergraduates and that those students would do better at less selective institutions (Elliott and others, 1996; Sowell, 1993; Thernstrom, 1995), while others have noted that the negative relationship between selectivity and success cannot simply be accounted for by the mismatch theory (Bonous-Hammarth, 2000; Chang, Cerna, Han, and Sàenz, 2008). Chang, Cerna, Han, and Sàenz, for example, analyzed a national sample of 2,964 students using logistic regression procedures. When controlling for a wide range of background and experiential variables, they found that Black, Hispanic, and Native American students have a 30 percent greater chance of leaving the biomedical or behavioral sciences if they attend an institution at which the average combined SAT score is 1100, compared with institutions where the average is 1000. They also found that attending an MSI was negatively associated with minority students' success. In their post hoc analysis, Chang, Cerna, Han, and Sàenz (2008) found that institutional selectively was negatively correlated with success at PWIs but positively associated with success at HBCUs, suggesting that greater institutional selectivity enhances the likelihood of success among racial and ethnic minority students in STEM who attend HBCUs. From this analysis, the authors concluded that the frequently cited negative relationship between institutional selectivity and minority students' success in STEM could be a function of the way highly selective institutions operate. That is, the low rates of success at those selective institutions could be the result of factors such as racial stereotypes in their campus climates and the competitive orientations of their campus cultures. We discuss these environmental factors further in the following sections.

In sum, the influences of MSIs and institutional selectivity on success among students of color in STEM are mixed and complex. Racial and ethnic minority students who attend HBCUs, and possibly other MSIs, are more likely to succeed than their peers who attend PWIs and less likely to succeed if they attend highly selective institutions than institutions of lower selectivity. Evidence suggests, however, that the predominantly White nature of highly selective institutions might be responsible for the negative impact of selectivity on success among students of color.

The Impact of Campus Environments

Much attention has been given to the influence of campus environments on racial and ethnic minority college students' success in general and minority students in STEM specifically. This section reviews evidence of the impact of two main aspects of the campus environment—campus climate and culture—on minority college students in STEM. First, because the words "climate" and "culture" are often conflated, recognizing the differences between these two concepts is important (Bauer, 1998). Kuh and Whitt (1988) examined the concept of culture in the context of higher education and defined it as the "collective, mutually shaping patterns of norms, values, practices, beliefs, and assumptions that guide the behavior of individuals and groups in higher education and provide a frame of reference within which to interpret the meaning of events and actions" (pp. 12–13). In addition, culture is, at least in part, a function of historical events, deeply embedded, and difficult to change (Peterson and Spencer, 1990; Schoenberg, 1992). Whereas campus culture refers to the *deeply embedded* patterns of values, beliefs, and assumptions, campus climate has been defined as the "*current* perceptions, attitudes, and expectations that define the institution and its members" (Bauer, 1998, p. 2). In contrast to campus culture, which is deeply entrenched in the history and fabric of an organization and difficult to alter, aspects of the campus climate are more malleable and frequently changing. When examining the experiences of minority students in STEM, it is important to understand the role of the campus climate and culture, as well as the climate and culture of STEM departments.

Campus and STEM Climates

More than twenty years ago, Moos (1986) developed a social and ecological model in an attempt to explain the influence of organizational climates on student development. He posited that personal (sociodemographic variables, expectations, personality, and coping skills) and environmental (physical, organizational, human aggregate, and climate) factors influence students' appraisal of their environment, their perceptions of potential coping responses, and their actual response to that environment. Students' responses determine the efforts that they make to adapt to or cope with their environment, which subsequently affects those students' stability and change. Baird (2000) applied the *appraisal* construct to explain how students' perceptions of the academic and social subsystems of the campus could be a key factor in their willingness and efforts to integrate into those subsystems. That is, students' appraisals of the climates of academic and social environments could be a central factor in their decisions to participate in various academic and social activities on their campuses. Not only does Baird's adaptation highlight the exclusion of important environmental variables in existing departure theory, but it also underscores the key links among campus climates, students' perceptions of those climates, and students' subsequent college experiences.

Central to Moos's model (1986) are the actual environment and students' perception of the environment. Thus while Moos's social and ecological model helps clarify the potential relationships between campus environments and students' experiences, it also can potentially further complicate our understanding of what constitutes campus climate. Naylor, Pritchard, and Ilgen (1980) addressed this potential problem by developing a schema to understand the various levels of an organization's climate. They asserted that the actual environmental attributes that influence students' perceptions (level one) are translated into individual perceptions of those attributes (level two), which in turn define the psychological climate construct (level three) that represents the degree of *friendliness* that the individual attaches to the climate. Baird (2000) noted that levels two and three are often conflated in higher education research. Nevertheless, Naylor, Pritchard, and Ilgen's model (1980) highlights the complexity of climates and the importance of considering both external and internal aspects of climate.

The role of campus climate in predicting students' success has received much attention in the research on racial and ethnic minority students (Berryman, 1983; Cabrera and others, 1999; Harper and Hurtado, 2007; Maple and Stage, 1991; Maramba, 2008b; Museus, Nichols, and Lambert, 2008; Nora and Cabrera, 1996; Sondgeroth and Stough, 1992). This research indicates that minority students often report chillier and less supportive campus climates than their White peers (Ancis, Sedlacek, and Mohr, 2000; Harper and Hurtado, 2007; Hurtado, 1992; Hurtado and others, 2007; Maramba, 2008b; Museus, Nichols, and Lambert, 2008; Nora and Cabrera, 1996; Rankin and Reason, 2005). That research also demonstrates that negative perceptions of the climate are associated with lower levels of adjustment, sense of belonging, institutional attachment, and success of students from all racial groups (Cabrera and others, 1999; Eimers and Pike, 1997; Hurtado and Carter, 1997; Hurtado, Carter, and Spuler, 1996; Nora and Cabrera, 1996; Pascarella and Terenzini,

2005). Although the broader campus climates in part shape the experiences of minority college students in STEM, climates in STEM departments are equally important.

Researchers who have examined the role of climate in the experiences of racial and ethnic minority students in STEM have found that those students report chilly and hostile climates at both two- and four-year institutions and that such environments can be associated with feelings of discouragement (Berryman, 1983; Fries-Britt, Younger, and Hall, 2010; Grandy, 1994; Maple and Stage, 1991; Oakes, 1990; Sondgeroth and Stough, 1992). Several studies also demonstrate that less supportive educational environments are related to Black, Hispanic, and Native American college students' departure from the STEM circuit (Bonous-Hammarth, 2000; Gloria and Kurpius, 2001; Grandy, 1998; Hurtado and others, 2007; Leslie, McClure, and Oaxaca, 1998). Although chilly and unsupportive climates are a salient factor that hinders students' success, the cultures of campuses and STEM departments and programs may present equally significant barriers for minority college students.

Campus and STEM Cultures

The most cited theory of student success in college is based on a cultural framework (Tinto, 1987, 1993). Tinto posited that students' level of integration into the academic and social systems of their respective campuses shapes those students' commitments to their goals and institution, which in turn determine their likelihood of persistence. The theory is based on Van Gennep's stages of cultural transition (1960). Specifically, Tinto borrowed Van Gennep's theoretical presupposition that students must dissociate from their traditional cultures and integrate into the cultures of their respective campus to successfully adjust to and persist through college. Tinto (1975) postulated that students must go through a stage of *separation,* during which they detach themselves from their cultures of origin (family and high school peers). According to Tinto, students then undergo a period of *transition,* which includes initial interactions with people in the cultures of their campus. The third stage of *incorporation* consists of the adoption of the cultural values and norms espoused by those in the culture of the college campus. Thus this theory posits that students who fail to sever ties with their communities of origin and integrate into their campus cultures are less likely to effectively adjust to the campus life and succeed in higher education.

Higher education scholars have questioned the applicability of Tinto's theory to explanations of racial and ethnic minority students' success (Braxton, 2000; Braxton, Sullivan, and Johnson, 1997; Hurtado and Carter, 1997; Kuh and Love, 2000; Museus and Quaye, 2009; Palmer, Davis, and Maramba, forthcoming *a*; Rendón, Jalomo, and Nora, 2000; Tierney, 1992). They argue that expecting minority students, many of whom come from cultures that are very different from those that exist at PWIs, to sever ties with their cultural heritage and assimilate to the culture of their campus places an unfair burden on those students and ignores institutional responsibility to facilitate racial and ethnic minority undergraduates' adjustment and success in college. Over the past decade, several alternative perspectives have emerged (Guiffrida, 2006; Kuh and Love, 2000; Museus and Quaye, 2009; Rendón, Jalomo, and Nora, 2000; Tierney, 1999). Rendón, Jalomo, and Nora, for example, applied the concept of bicultural socialization to an understanding of how racial and ethnic minority students can learn how to effectively navigate multiple cultures simultaneously. And building on the work of Kuh and Love (2000), Museus and Quaye (2009) generated an intercultural framework of minority students' persistence that emphasizes the importance of both collective (subcultures such as academic programs and student organizations on campus) and individual (faculty members and peers) agents fostering connections with minority students.

These new perspectives have several things in common. They indicate that culture matters in the success of racial and ethnic minority college students. Those perspectives also suggest that minority students may face increased difficulty connecting to the cultures of predominantly White college campuses because they come from home cultures that are very different from those found on their campuses, and institutions can have a positive impact on the success of racial and ethnic minority students by creating meaningful connections between campus cultures and minority undergraduates and by validating the cultural backgrounds of those students.

Cultural alienation, marginalization, and isolation. Few researchers have examined how campus culture influences racial and ethnic minority students' success in higher education (Museus and Harris, 2010). The evidence that does exist in this area suggests that racial and ethnic minority students in STEM fields also experience difficulty connecting to and navigating the cultures of their campuses. Specifically, minority students do in fact experience alienation, marginalization, and isolation from the cultures of PWIs (Allen, 1992; Davis, 1994; Fries-Britt and Turner, 2002; Green and Glasson, 2009; Gonzalez, 2003; Feagin, Vera, and Imani, 1996; Sondgeroth and Stough, 1992; White and Shelley, 1996). Alternatively, institutions that have more collective orientations and humanized environments may positively influence the outcomes of racial and ethnic minorities at two- and four-year institutions (Museus and Liverman, 2010). Empirical research in this area also indicates that racial and ethnic minority undergraduates can find membership in cultural enclaves (that is, subcultures) that can protect them from the larger unfriendly environments of campus and facilitate their success in higher education (see, for example, Gonzalez, 2003; Guiffrida, 2003; Harper and Quaye, 2007; Kiang, 2002; Museus, 2008b).

Cultural stereotypes. Multiple cultural factors could contribute to the barriers that prevent minority students from connecting to their campuses or STEM departments. For example, research on minority students has underscored the fact that stereotypes of Blacks as academically inferior in the campus and classroom environment can place immense pressure on them (Fries-Britt and Turner, 2001; Lewis, Chesler, and Forman, 2000; Museus, 2008a) that can negatively influence their engagement and academic performance (Museus, 2008a; Steele, 1999). This stereotype has been identified as a critical barrier to the success of minority students in general and in STEM majors specifically (Brown, 2004; Cote and Levin, 1997; Green and Glasson, 2009; Moore, 2000; Steele, 1999). Compounding this reality is the fact that stereotypes of science as a Western construct can cause minority students to adopt negative perceptions of themselves in STEM environments (Brand, Glasson, and Green, 2006). Thus, Brown (2004) highlighted the importance of combating the cultural influences that negatively affect Black students' perceptions of their own capabilities in STEM. Although Brown focused on Black students, it could be an equally important consideration for Hispanics and Native Americans.

Individualist and competitive cultural values. Another aspect of campus and STEM cultures that could create challenges for racial and ethnic minority students is the individualistic and competitive values of some institutions and STEM departments (Guiffrida, 2006; Museus and Harris, 2010). Many minority college students originate from cultures that are more collectively oriented than Western cultures (Fisk, Kitayama, Markus, and Nisbett, 1998; Guiffrida, 2006; Triandis, McCuster, and Hui, 1990), and researchers have noted that collectivist orientations might contribute to environments conducive to success among racial and ethnic minority students (Guiffrida, 2006; Museus and Harris, 2010). In contrast, however, the cultures of STEM departments are often described as individualistic and competitive, conflicting with the cultural orientations from which many minority students come. One manifestation of this individualist and competitive cultural orientation is the gatekeeper courses that weed out students who are allegedly not sufficiently academically prepared (Massey, 1992; Seymour and Hewitt, 1997). The fact that STEM departments perpetuate such individualist and competitive cultures is important, especially because minority students are less likely to receive adequate preparation, putting them at a disadvantage in such courses (Elliott and others, 1996; Green and Glasson, 2009; Maton, Hrabowski, and Schmitt, 2000; Ramist, Lewis, and McCamley-Jenkins, 1994). Given the purpose of courses in weeding out unprepared students and the fact that racial and ethnic minority students are less prepared for STEM majors on average, it is no surprise that such courses are often described by these students as difficult (Duderstadt, 1990; Gainen, 1995; Treisman, 1992) and can deter them from pursuing or continuing to pursue STEM degrees.

In sum, institutional environments are a major factor influencing the experiences and outcomes of racial and ethnic minority college students in STEM. Both the climates and cultures of predominantly White campuses and STEM departments pose several challenges for these students, suggesting that many of the challenges encountered by minority students are deeply embedded in the fabric of college campuses and STEM fields.

The Impact of Institutional Agents

Earlier in this chapter, we mentioned the importance of individual campus cultural agents such as faculty members, academic advisors, or peers in facilitating racial and ethnic minority students' connections to the cultures of their campuses. Weidman (1989) posited that faculty and peers shape undergraduate students' perceptions of and experiences in college. He also asserted that, through these interactions, students develop negative or positive appraisals of the college experience. As previously mentioned, other theoretical perspectives also underscore the importance of students' fostering connections with institutional agents on campus (Kuh and Love, 2000; Museus and Quaye, 2009; Rendón, Jalomo, and Nora, 2000). Connections to campus agents are the strongest predictors of success among college students in general (Pascarella and Terenzini, 1991, 2005), and evidence suggests that they also play a critical role in the success of racial and ethnic minority students (Cole and Barber, 2003; Feagin, Vera, and Imani, 1996; Fleming, 1984; Fries-Britt and Turner, 2002; Gloria, Castellanos, Lopez, and Rosales, 2005; Hernandez, 2000; Jackson, Smith, and Hill, 2003; Museus and Neville, forthcoming; Museus and Quaye, 2009; Palmer and Gasman, 2008; Pascarella and Terenzini, 2005; Sedlacek, 1987) as well as minority students in STEM fields specifically (Chang, 2002; Cole and Espinoza, 2008; Farrell, 2002; Fries-Britt, Younger, and Hall, 2010; Grandy, 1998; Hrabowski and Maton, 2009; Palmer, Davis, and Thompson, 2010; Treisman, 1992). This section reviews the role of institutional agents in the experiences of minority students in STEM.

The Influence of Faculty

Existing literature indicates that faculty play a critical role in predicting the success of racial and ethnic minority students in STEM. Research on minority students in general demonstrates that faculty can have both a negative and positive impact on racial and ethnic minority students' experiences and outcomes (Ceja and Rhodes, 2004; Feagin, Vera, and Imani, 1996; Guiffrida, 2003; Museus and Neville, forthcoming; Palmer and Gasman, 2008; Palmer, Maramba, and Holmes, forthcoming; Solórzano, Ceja, and Yosso, 2000). For example, Solórzano, Ceja, and Yosso (2000) conducted a qualitative study of

Black undergraduates at a PWI and reported how faculty showed subtle forms of prejudice and discrimination toward those students. Conversely, Museus and Neville (forthcoming) examined individual interviews with sixty AAPI, Black, and Hispanic students across four institutions and discovered that faculty and other institutional agents (advisors, counselors, and student affairs staff) who shared common ground with students humanized the educational experience, provided holistic support, and were proactive in serving minority students had a positive influence on those participants' success by connecting those undergraduates with important information and support on campus. Specifically in STEM, research shows that the absence of minority faculty who can function as role models for racial and ethnic minority students, faculty with insufficient preparation, and faculty who maintain low expectations for racial and ethnic minority students can hinder their success in college (Agosto, Gasson, and Atwood, 2008; Cole and Espinoza, 2008; Fries-Britt, Younger, and Hall, 2010; Gloria, Castellanos, Lopez, and Rosales, 2005; Hernandez, 2000; Grandy, 1998; Green, 1978; Perna and others, 2009; Seymour and Hewitt, 1997). But faculty interaction, support, and encouragement have all been linked to racial and ethnic minority students' success in STEM (Cole and Espinoza, 2008; Grandy, 1994; Hernandez and Lopez, 2004–05; Hrabowski and Maton, 2009; Johnson, 2007; Leslie, McClure, and Oaxaca, 1998).

Faculty members in STEM also exert an important influence on the success of minority students by way of their pedagogical approaches (see, for example, MacDonald and Korinek, 1995; Seymour and Hewitt, 1997; Sondgeroth and Stough, 1992). Four pedagogy-related factors seem to have an impact on the success of racial and ethnic minority students in STEM: (1) small and interactive classrooms, (2) collaborative learning, (3) a diverse and culturally responsive curriculum, and (4) a curriculum relevant to real-world problems. First, STEM courses have historically been based on large lecture-based courses, which have a negative influence on the experiences of minority students (Brown, 2002; Johnson, 2007). Alternatively, smaller and more interactive classes have been associated with success among racial and ethnic minority students in STEM (Brown, 2002; Perna and others, 2009). Second, researchers have found collaborative learning—work in small groups through which students solve problems while the instructor facilitates the collaborative work—to significantly and positively influence professional competencies, development, analytical thinking skills, and success (Cabrera, Colbeck, and Terenzini, 2001; Cabrera and others, 2002; Treisman, 1992). Third, several scholars have discussed the problematic lack of cultural relevance in the STEM curriculum and the need for faculty to address this reality (Farrell, 2002; Perna and others, 2009; Jarosz, 2003) and the absence of STEM curricula that is pertinent to real-world issues (Davis and Finelli, 2007). Thus, implementing curricula that are relevant to both cultural backgrounds and real-world problems has been noted as critical to increasing the success of racial and ethnic minority students in STEM. We discuss the impact of such efforts on minority undergraduates later in this chapter.

Finally, evidence suggests that faculty members' engagement of students in undergraduate research can have a positive impact on student outcomes in STEM (Barlow and Villarejo, 2004; Hurtado and others, 2009; Lopatto, 2004; Strayhorn, 2010). National data also reveal, however, that racial and ethnic minority students—Black undergraduates, specifically—are significantly less likely to participate in such opportunities (Hurtado and others, 2008). Thus, disparities in access to such important opportunities in college are an important consideration.

The Influence of Academic Advisors

Existing literature indicates that academic advising is associated with college students' success (Pascarella and Terenzini, 2005) and that humanized, proactive, and holistic academic advising can contribute to institutions' effectiveness in fostering success among minority students (Museus and Ravello, 2010). Despite the potential positive impact of academic advising, whether advisors contribute to racial and ethnic minority students' success in STEM fields is unclear. Research on racial and ethnic minorities in STEM, however, does indicate that poor advising can negatively influence persistence in the STEM circuit, but that research is qualitative in nature and not generalizable (Seymour and Hewitt, 1997). Nevertheless, this evidence that inadequate academic advising can be associated with leaving the STEM circuit may be one reason that STEM-specific opportunity and support programs incorporate academic advising into their services (see, for example, Maton, Hrabowski, and Schmitt, 2000; Maton and Hrabowski, 2004).

Researchers have noted the potential utility of intrusive academic advising. Intrusive advising is based on the practice of advisors' meeting with students several times throughout the academic year (Tsui, 2007). Empirical research suggests that such practices can and do have an impact on racial and ethnic minority college students' success (Glennen and Baxley, 1985; Museus and Ravello, 2010). Glennen and Baxley found that intrusive advising was associated with higher first-year retention, better grades, and more completed courses. Research on the impact of intrusive practices in advising minority students in STEM majors, however, is difficult to find. Thus, the effects of intrusive advising on success in STEM is a critical area for future research.

The Influence of Peers

Peers exert one of the most powerful, if not the most salient, influences on college students' experiences and outcomes in general (Astin, 1993; Pascarella and Terenzini, 1991, 2005). Indeed, decades of research indicate that involvement in formal and informal activities with peers is positively associated with success. It is through such involvement that racial and ethnic minority students find supportive environments on campus (Guiffrida, 2003; Harper and Quaye, 2007; Maramba and Velasquez, forthcoming; Museus, 2008b; Palmer, Davis, and Maramba, forthcoming *b*). Research has shown that peers have a profound impact on the experiences and outcomes of racial and ethnic minority college students in STEM as well (Bonous-Hammarth, 2000; Cole and Barber, 2003; Cross and Vick, 2001; Hurtado and others, 2007; Johnson, 2007). The relationship is a bit more complicated, however, when examining students in STEM specifically.

The empirical research on the impact of peers on racial and ethnic minority students' success in STEM indicates that the *type* of interaction that students have with their peers does matter. Cole and Espinoza (2008), for example, conducted a longitudinal study of 146 Hispanic students in STEM and found that involvement in diversity functions and studying with other students was negatively associated with their GPA. These findings could be due to the fact that such involvement, if it is outside the STEM environment, can marginalize minority students from the cultures of STEM disciplines

(Bonous-Hammarth, 2000). For instance, spending time at diversity functions could prevent racial and ethnic minority students in STEM from studying enough to pass math and science gatekeeper courses. In contrast, when minority students are involved in preprofessional clubs in STEM, they are more likely to persist (Chang, Cerna, Han, and Sàenz, 2008; Hurtado and others, 2007). In addition, when studying in STEM-related peer groups, working with peers in science laboratories, and sharing information with upperclassmen, racial and ethnic minorities are more likely to succeed (Fries-Britt, Younger, and Hall, 2010; Treisman, 1992).

As we mentioned in the previous chapter, evidence might suggest that peers can also facilitate minority students' success by serving the important function of role modeling (Bandura, 1997; Murphey, 1995, 1996; Weiten, Lashley, and Lloyd, 1991). More specifically, when students observe peer role models succeed in STEM fields, they can observe that they have the potential to succeed in STEM as well (Brown and Inouye, 1978; Murphey and Arao, 2001). Researchers have also underscored the importance of students' and their peer role models' sharing important social characteristics such as race (Murphey, 1995, 1996), because those similarities enhance the message that the observer is capable of achieving the same task as the role model. Thus, minority students who are academically successful can send messages to their minority peers that the latter can succeed as well. Again, however, empirical research on the effects of peer role modeling on minority students' success in STEM is lacking.

In sum, campus agents have a powerful impact on the success of minority students in STEM. The nature of the impact, however, depends on the quality and quantity of interactions that students have with various faculty, advisors, and peers on campus, with many of those interactions facilitating success and some potentially hindering it. What is clear is that the relationship between interactions and success might be different for racial and ethnic minority students in STEM fields than for those in non-STEM majors.

The Impact of Psychological Factors

A person's "motivational system" comprises several factors, including their interest, self-efficacy, and goals in a particular domain (Ford, 1992). The previous chapter underscored how interest and self-efficacy in STEM develop during the precollege years and influence progress in the STEM circuit. This section highlights the fact that these variables continue to influence the success of racial and ethnic minority students in STEM. Indeed, self-concept, self-efficacy, interests, ambition, commitment to STEM, and aspirations and expectations to earn a STEM degree have been associated with success in the STEM circuit (Anderson, 1990; Chang, Cerna, Han, and Sàenz, 2008; Gloria and Kurpius, 2001; Grandy, 1998; Hackett, Betz, Casas, and Rocha-Singh, 1992; Hernandez and Lopez, 2004–05; Hilton, Hsia, Solórzano, and Benton, 1989; Huang, Taddese, Walter, and Peng, 2000; Hurtado and others, 2007; Jackson, Gardner, and Sullivan, 1993; Leslie, McClure, and Oaxaca, 1998; Waller, 2006).

Self-concept, or how one perceives himself or herself, and self-efficacy, the belief in one's ability to accomplish a goal, are two of the most-cited psychological factors attributed to participation and success among minority college students in STEM majors. Specifically, higher levels of self-concept and self-efficacy are associated with a greater likelihood of entering science or math fields, personal commitment to science and math, and higher levels of adjustment, performance, and success among these students (see, for example, Anderson, 1990, 1996; Gerardi, 2005; Grandy, 1998; Hackett, Betz, Casas, and Rocha-Singh, 1992; Hernandez and Lopez, 2004–05; Jackson, Gardner, and Sullivan, 1993; Leslie, McClure, and Oaxaca, 1998).

The research on self-concept and self-efficacy is related to our earlier discussion about cultural stereotypes. We discussed the salience of stereotypes that imply that racial and ethnic minority students, except AAPIs, are inferior (Museus, 2008a). Such stereotypes can cause racial and ethnic minority college students to feel inferior in STEM fields (see, for example, Brand, Glasson, and Green, 2006; Howard and Hammond, 1985). Moreover, Black undergraduates who perceive their race or ethnicity as inferior are less likely to succeed academically in general and in STEM in particular (Brown, 2004; Green and Glasson, 2009; Hall-Greene, 2000; Steele, 1999).

In sum, psychological factors play an important role in determining racial and ethnic minority student outcomes in STEM. Moreover, the relationships among these psychological factors might be complex. Although most research in this area employs methods that do not permit the examination of complex indirect effects, Waller (2006) used path analytic techniques to demonstrate that self-efficacy in math might predict expectations, interests, intentions, and choices in math. Much remains to be learned, however, about the process by which environmental constructs interact with these factors to influence success.

The Impact of STEM-Specific Opportunity and Support Programs

This section provides an overview of STEM-specific programs that are designed to serve underrepresented college students in the STEM fields. Unlike the initiatives that we reviewed in the previous chapter, which are designed to increase interest and enrollment in STEM majors in college, the programs discussed in this section are aimed at providing opportunities (such as undergraduate research) and support (such as faculty mentors and peer study groups) for students who are already enrolled in STEM majors. These programs vary widely in terms of the type of institution where they are located, the majors that they include, and the racial groups that they serve. They offer a wide range of services, including financial support, summer bridge opportunities, mentoring, undergraduate research, academic advising, tutoring, and career counseling–oriented programs. Nevertheless, all of these programs are in some way aimed at increasing success among racial and ethnic minority students in STEM.

Although we acknowledge that general targeted support programs on college campuses serve underrepresented students in both STEM and non-STEM fields and can positively impact the experiences and outcomes of racial and ethnic minority students in STEM (Museus, 2010a), we focus on STEM-specific programs aimed at promoting minority college students' success. Although few methodologically rigorous assessments of STEM-specific opportunity and support programs in higher education have been published (Gándara and Maxwell-Jolly, 1999), a handful of studies assess these programs' impact on student outcomes. This section focuses on these programs that have been the focus of empirical literature while acknowledging that this list is not exhaustive and many other programs exist that have not been empirically evaluated using rigorous research methods (see, for example, Institute for Higher

Education Policy, 2009; White, Altschuld, and Lee, 2008). We caution again that these studies are limited, as they do not assess which aspects of these programs are or are not effective.

The Mathematics Workshop Program

One of the earliest STEM-specific programs discussed in the literature is the Mathematics Workshop Program (MWP), created in 1978 at the University of California, Berkeley. The MWP is based on research conducted by Uri Treisman, who conducted qualitative research to examine the disparity in achievement between Chinese and Black students in mathematics (Fullilove and Treisman, 1990). He concluded that a primary reason that Chinese students studied more hours and performed significantly better than their Black counterparts was that they studied in groups. The group work was associated with several benefits: (1) Chinese students studied fourteen hours per week, compared with eight hours for Black students, (2) when no group members could solve a problem, they concluded that the problem was complicated enough to seek help, (3) the study groups facilitated the exchange of information among peers. These findings provided the foundation for the MWP.

The MWP is an honors program with participants from all racial and ethnic groups, but a majority (80 percent) of students in the program are Black or Hispanic undergraduates (Fullilove and Treisman, 1990). Students participate in study groups that correspond with lectures and consist of five to seven people. Fullilove and Treisman compared MWP participants and nonparticipants on multiple outcome measures and found involvement in the program to be associated with improved math course grades and degree completion. They also found that MWP participants significantly outperformed nonparticipants with stronger academic backgrounds (based on SAT scores). Their subsequent qualitative analyses generated several findings: (1) the MWP creates academically oriented peer groups that value math achievement and success, (2) participants spend more time studying (ten to fourteen hours) compared with nonparticipants (six to eight hours), and (3) MWP students acquire important social and study skills from interaction with their peer groups. Several questions about the MWP remain, however, including questions about whether certain subgroups of students benefit more than others from the program. For example, it is unclear whether low-income minority students, who are more likely to face greater pressure to work longer hours during college and have less time available to study in groups, benefit from programs like the MWP as much as their more affluent peers.

The Meyerhoff Program

The Meyerhoff Program was established in 1988 and is focused on increasing success among Black students in STEM at the University of Maryland, Baltimore County (UMBC). The program emphasizes four areas: knowledge and skills, motivation and support, monitoring and advising, and academic and social involvement (Hrabowski and Maton, 1995). It also consists of a summer bridge program, study groups, program community, counseling, tutoring, summer research internships, administrative and faculty involvement, community and family involvement, and mentors. Admission into the Meyerhoff Program is selective. Principals and counselors throughout Maryland nominate approximately fourteen hundred students for the program, and approximately forty to sixty students are selected, equaling an acceptance rate of 3 to 4 percent (Maton, Hrabowski, and Schmitt, 2000). In terms of academic qualifications, Meyerhoff participants had average SAT math scores of 657 and SAT verbal scores of 623 and did not receive a grade lower than a B in any math or science course during high school.

Researchers have found this program to be associated with higher grade point averages than those of students who did not participate in the program (Hrabowski and Maton, 1995; Maton, Hrabowski, and Schmitt, 2000). Hrabowski and Maton, for example, compared three Meyerhoff Program cohorts with historical cohorts at UMBC (before the Meyerhoff Program) who met the entrance requirements for the program. They found that the Meyerhoff cohorts had higher grade point averages in the first year of college than their preprogram counterparts. To assess the long-term effects of the Meyerhoff Program on academic achievement, Maton, Hrabowski, and Schmitt (2000) subsequently compared the outcomes of Meyerhoff Program participants with historical UMBC cohorts and students who were accepted into the program but declined and attended colleges and universities elsewhere. Meyerhoff participants had higher academic performance, science and engineering degree completion, and graduate school attendance rates than the comparison samples. These findings must be interpreted with caution because this study was not conducted using an experimental design, and it is unclear whether Meyerhoff students succeed at significantly higher rates than other UMBC students with similar academic backgrounds, qualifications, and motivations.

The Emerging Scholars Program

In 1988, the same year that the Meyerhoff Program came into existence, the Emerging Scholars Program (ESP) began at the University of Texas at Austin (Moreno and Muller, 1999). Similar to the Meyerhoff Program, the ESP is aimed at challenging high-achieving students to excel in mathematics. For example, the ESP focuses on serving students with SAT math scores above 500 who graduated in the top 10 to 20 percent of their graduating class in high school. In addition, similar to the Mathematics Workshop Program, the ESP takes into account the importance of peer groups in fostering success; the aim of the ESP is to increase diversity among students in mathematics by facilitating first-year calculus students' success through the creation of diverse support groups in which students can share knowledge. The ESP has several components:

Two-hour workshops, three times a week, compared with non-ESP students, who attend one-hour sessions two times a week;

A focus on collaborative problem solving in the workshops; and

The development of friendship groups through participation in small-group workshops.

The ESP is open to undergraduates of all racial backgrounds, and although the program at Austin is the largest and longest-running ESP in the nation, Emerging Scholars Programs can be found at other universities across the nation. What might be unique about the ESP at Austin is that it focuses on facilitating students' successful completion of a specific gatekeeper course—calculus.

Moreno and Muller (1999) analyzed a sample of more than fifteen hundred Black, Hispanic, and White first- and second-year students who took calculus between 1988 and 1994 using ordinary least squares and logistic regression procedures to determine whether participation in the ESP was associated with students' success. The authors demonstrated that participation in the ESP is associated with several positive outcomes. Specifically, they found that, compared with non-ESP participants, ESP participants earned significantly higher calculus grades and were more likely to enroll in a second semester of calculus. They also concluded that participation in the ESP might also indirectly and positively influence choosing a major in science, mathematics, and engineering through the program's positive influence on calculus grades.

Biology Undergraduate Scholars Program

Another promising STEM-specific opportunity and support program that incorporates undergraduate research in its efforts to support and facilitate success among racial and ethnic minority students is the Biology Undergraduate Scholars Program (BUSP) at the University of California, Davis, which was established in 1988 to address racial and ethnic disparities in the biological sciences. The program's design was informed by literature on college students' success (Astin, 1982; Astin and Astin, 1992; Wilson, 2000) and existing minority student support programs, and it is focused on addressing minority students' departure through the implementation of structural and pedagogical changes. Specifically, the BUSP is aimed at providing academic, financial, and support services to students of color. The BUSP offers its participants several features:

Supplemental instruction in general chemistry, calculus, and biology;

Academic and personal advising;

Voluntary laboratory research experience, which also results in financial support;

The development of peer support networks (Barlow and Villarejo, 2004).

Barlow and Villarejo (2004) assessed the impact of the BUSP on undergraduate outcomes. Controlling for demographic variables and academic preparation, they conducted multivariate regression analyses using a sample of 397 BUSP students. Their results indicated that BUSP participants had greater odds of persisting in math and science courses and graduating in biology than nonparticipants. The authors also concluded that program participants who specifically took part in the optional laboratory research experience of the program were more likely to pursue graduate school than undergraduates at the same university who did not participate in the experiences. The authors also reported that half of the participants indicated that research experiences influenced their choice of major and that 59 percent reported that it influenced their choice of career. Half the students who indicated that research experiences influenced their choice of major, however, also reported that those experiences deterred them from further laboratory involvement. This finding underscores an important gap in knowledge regarding what type of research experiences negatively influence students. Such information could help inform the development of more effective STEM support programs.

Summer Undergraduate Research Program

Programs primarily focused on providing undergraduates with research experiences have been an increasingly popular way to attract students to and help them succeed in the STEM fields. One such program is the Summer Undergraduate Research Program (SURP), which was created in 1989 at the University of Minnesota's Twin Cities campus (Walters, 1997). Requirements for participating in the SURP include completion of basic biology, chemistry, and physics courses as well as a grade point average of 3.2 or above. The SURP is designed to give students the opportunity to conduct research in the biological sciences; it serves a diverse array of students, including AAPI, Black, Hispanic, Native American, and White undergraduates. Students are required to commit to involvement in two months of research, which include four activities:

Assisting faculty members on their research projects;

Executing independent research projects;

Participating in seminars that complement the research; and

Summarizing and presenting research findings to the campus community.

Walters (1997) conducted qualitative interviews with fourteen individuals (five Black, five Hispanic, and four White) who participated in the SURP. All participants reported that the program had a positive influence on their experiences and decisions to attend graduate programs in STEM. The sample comprised purposefully selected gifted and talented students, however, so it is unclear whether these students were already motivated to the extent that they maximized the benefits of the SURP that might be uncharacteristic of the majority of SURP participants. Walters reported that statistical analyses suggested that programmatic factors affected participants' choices about graduate and professional school, but details were not reported.

Walters failed to report information regarding least effective aspects of the program. She did state that "few disappointments with the program or frustrations about the program structure were expressed" (p. 26) but did not provide any further details. She explained that participants' lack of reported disappointment or frustration could be the result of the sampling bias, which, again, could highlight the need for researchers to explore the perspectives and experiences of those who have dropped out or been dissatisfied with their STEM program experiences to uncover the aspects of these initiatives that are least effective or could be improved.

The Undergraduate Research Opportunity Program
The Undergraduate Research Opportunity Program (UROP) at the University of Michigan was also formed in 1989 (Davis, and Finelli, 2007). Originally designed for underrepresented students, the UROP expanded to serving about twelve hundred first- and second-year students from all racial and ethnic backgrounds. The program consists of two primary components: regular meetings with peer advisors who are graduates of the UROP and participation in the research process. Regarding the latter, students conduct literature searches, participate in laboratory experiences, and present the results of their research. Davis and Finelli note that the UROP serves students from various departments across the university's campus but that it is in high demand among engineering students.

Researchers have studied the impact of the UROP and found that it is positively associated with higher levels of engagement, academic performance, and persistence (Gregerman, 1999; Hathaway, 2003; Hathaway, Nagda, and Gregerman, 2002; Nagda and others, 1998). Although research suggests trivial differences when comparing the persistence of UROP and non-UROP students

(Hathaway, 2003; Nagda and others, 1998), disaggregated analyses also reveal that, although program participation did not yield significant effects for White students, racial and ethnic minority undergraduates who participated in the UROP were significantly more likely to persist than their non-UROP counterparts.

In addition to the UROP, the University of Michigan houses other initiatives, including a service-learning course in the first-year engineering curriculum that is in part designed to reveal the human aspects of engineering and make it relevant to students of color toward the end of increasing diversity in the field and an initiative to increase the real-world context of an introductory engineering course (Davis and Finelli, 2007). Quasi-experimental studies suggest that these initiatives also have a positive impact on outcomes such as satisfaction and academic performance (Burn and Holloway, 2006; Meadows and Jarema, 2006).

In sum, several STEM opportunity and support programs have been created to foster success among racial and ethnic minority students in STEM in higher education. A handful of them have been evaluated using rigorous qualitative and quantitative methods, and those assessments have generally found a positive relationship between programmatic interventions and racial and ethnic minority students' success in STEM fields. Much remains to be learned about the positive, and potentially negative, impact that these programs and various aspects of these initiatives can have on minority students' experiences and outcomes. It should be noted again that our list is not exhaustive and that other programs have been examined and found to have an impact on outcomes such as mathematical and scientific reasoning, achievement, and retention (Good, Halpin, and Halpin, 2002a, 2002b).

Conclusion

Existing empirical research has uncovered several factors that influence the success of racial and ethnic minority students once they have entered higher education: financial influences such as ability to pay for college, the type of institution a student attends (whether minority serving or selective), campus and STEM environments, institutional agents, and psychological factors.

Existing literature also indicates that STEM-specific opportunity and support programs—which are designed to positively shape these factors by cultivating more positive environments, quality interactions with faculty and peers, and students' interest and self-efficacy in STEM fields—have been found to influence the success of racial and ethnic minority students in STEM in postsecondary education.

Implications for Future Research, Policy, and Practice in STEM Education

T HE FIRST CHAPTER OF THIS VOLUME underscored the importance of maximizing human potential, cultivating success among racial
and ethnic minority students in the STEM education circuit, and increasing
the number of postsecondary degree recipients and qualified professionals in
the STEM fields. We based these urgent goals on two interrelated trends:
increases in the proportion of the national population that is from racial and
ethnic minority backgrounds and the continuing racial and ethnic disparities
from which racial and ethnic minorities in STEM suffer. As a result of these
trends, it is timely for policymakers and practitioners to cultivate greater success among Americans who can stabilize the nation's competitiveness by intro-
ducing scientific and technological innovations to the world.

The second and third chapters identified and discussed the factors that
negatively and positively influence racial and ethnic minority students' success in the STEM circuit. Specifically, we synthesized the literature on minority students in STEM to delineate the conditions under and extent to which
those individuals are able to enter and persist through the STEM education
circuit and complete a baccalaureate degree in STEM fields.

This chapter focuses on two tasks. First, given the depth and breadth of
K–12 and college-level factors that facilitate, moderate, or constrain success
among racial and ethnic minority students in STEM, we constructed the
Racial and Ethnic Minorities in STEM (REM STEM) Model to offer readers
a visual depiction of our synthesis and analysis of the literature (see Figure 12).
The REM STEM Model illustrates the process by which various factors influence racial and ethnic minority students' success in the STEM education circuit

Figure 12
The Racial and Ethnic Minorities in STEM Model

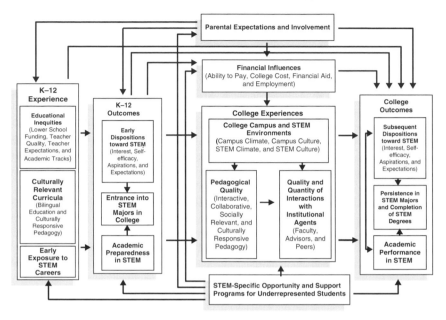

as well as the complex relationships that exist among those variables. Second, we draw from our synthesis to delineate implications for future research, policy, and practice in STEM education.

The Racial and Ethnic Minorities in STEM Model

The REM STEM Model illustrates the process by which critical factors influence racial and ethnic minority students' progress though the STEM circuit from the early years of elementary school through completion of a college degree. The REM STEM Model includes seven primary constructs, some of which comprise multiple components. The first construct on the left includes *K–12 experience* variables that influence minority students' K–12 outcomes, and it consists of three components. The first component of this construct, *educational inequities*, refers to the influence of systemic structural inequalities from which minority students suffer because of their racial and socioeconomic backgrounds such as lower levels of funding for schools, disproportionate numbers of unqualified teachers, lower teacher expectations, and channels that track lower academic ability. The second component, *culturally relevant curricula,* includes the availability of bilingual education and culturally responsive pedagogy. Third, salient K–12 experiences include students' *early exposure to STEM careers.*

The REM STEM Model posits that all three of these K–12 experience factors affect the second main construct in the model—*K–12 outcomes*, which include *academic preparedness in STEM, dispositions toward STEM* (self-efficacy, interest, and aspirations and expectations) and *entrance into STEM majors in college.* Moreover, K–12 outcomes influence the third and fourth constructs in the model—racial and ethnic minority students' *college experiences* (the environments they experience, the quality of pedagogy they receive, and the quality and quantity of their interactions with various agents on campus) and *college outcomes* (subsequent dispositions toward STEM fields, academic performance in STEM, and success in STEM in college).

Three other constructs are displayed at the top and bottom of the model. *Financial influences* such as racial and ethnic minority students' ability to pay for college are partially shaped by students' K–12 outcomes, particularly in terms of determining students' access to merit aid. Finances partially shape their college experience (for example, students who must work many hours do not have the time to interact with faculty outside class in meaningful ways) and outcomes (those students' achieving worse grades than if they did not have to work many hours). The *parental expectations and involvement* construct influences students' K–12 experiences, K–12 precollege outcomes, ability to pay for college, and college outcomes. And *STEM-specific opportunity and support programs* can influence racial and ethnic minority students' K–12 outcomes, parental expectations and involvement, ability to pay for college, college experiences, and postsecondary outcomes.

Each construct illustrated and described above may be informative to researchers, policymakers, and practitioners who wish to understand the factors that influence racial and ethnic minority students' success in the STEM circuit. The K–12 variables in the model are critically important to cultivate racial and ethnic minority students' interests, aspirations, and self-efficacy toward STEM education. The college-level factors are important in efforts to generate higher levels of persistence toward the completion of a degree in a STEM major among racial and ethnic minority students. The relationships between these constructs are related to the implications for research, policy, and practice to which we now turn.

Implications for Future Research

Our preceding literature review and emergent model have several implications for future research. First, sponsors of large databases should account for the within-race differences we describe in this volume when constructing national surveys. Such changes in the ways data are collected could be initiated by the U.S. Department of Education's National Center for Education Statistics or other national research centers that administer large national surveys. Similarly, researchers who employ qualitative traditions to answer questions related to racial and ethnic minority students' success in STEM should illuminate the heterogeneity in racial groups. Such disaggregation is critical for developing more contextualized and complex understandings of the experiences and outcomes of minority students because different subgroups have varying foundations and experiences in educational contexts. For example, Fries-Britt, Younger, and Hall (2010) found that international Black students and Black Americans understand campus cultures and climates in physics departments differently. More specifically, although most Black students from the Caribbean and African countries believed that African Americans were hypersensitive to racial issues, African Americans believed that international Black students overlooked those important issues because they did not fully understand American society. Accounting for within-race differences, such as the citizenship, ethnic, and socioeconomic diversity in AAPI, Black, Hispanic, and Native American communities, is an underdeveloped line of inquiry and critical area for future research. Such research is necessary for advancing existing levels of knowledge about these populations in STEM education and can help educators understand how to serve all racial and ethnic minority students most effectively.

A second implication for research centers on the need for a better understanding of the role of parental engagement in racial and ethnic minority students' educational experiences and outcomes in the STEM circuit. Specifically, evidence about the types of parental engagement that contribute to students' success in STEM is needed to help teachers understand how to most effectively engage both the minority students and their parents. How and under what conditions are parents able to help students become academically successful in mathematics and science? How do teachers engage parents in a way that gives those parents the tools to help their children develop and even master skills in mathematics and science early in students' educational experience? These lines of inquiry are critical to advance our understanding of practices that contribute to racial and ethnic minority students' success in STEM.

Third, a gap is apparent in the knowledge base regarding how school or institutional type affects racial and ethnic minority students' success in the STEM circuit. In K–12, what roles do charter schools play in preparing racial and ethnic minority students for STEM majors in college? Do model K–12 schools and programs exist that would encourage replication? Alternatively, at the postsecondary level, what impact does attending a Hispanic-serving institution have on racial and ethnic minorities' success in the STEM circuit? What aspects of the environment at HBCUs are the most powerful predictors of undergraduates' success at those institutions? Finally, what specific aspects of highly selective colleges and universities hinder success among racial and ethnic minority students in STEM? Chang, Cerna, Han, and Sàenz (2008) noted that, although highly selective institutions have the reputation and resources that can aid in fostering success among minority students, they could also be creating an environment that inhibits those students' progress through the STEM circuit. They suggest that some of the environmental factors that might contribute to this situation are their highly competitive orientations, their focus on research, and the absence of role models of racial and ethnic minority backgrounds. Future research should examine the extent to which these and other factors contribute to the low rates of success among minority undergraduates at highly selective institutions.

A fourth important area for future research is the experiences and outcomes of racial and ethnic minority students in STEM at community colleges. Our synthesis and analysis of literature disproportionately focused on four-year institutions because the vast majority of empirical research has been conducted at four-year colleges and universities. Given that such a large number of racial and ethnic minority students attend community colleges (Chapa and De La Rosa, 2006), these institutions play a critical role in the STEM circuit. Malcom (2010), for example, analyzed national data from the National Survey of Recent College Graduates and concluded that more than 60 percent of Latinos who earned a bachelor's degree in STEM had attended a community college at some point in their college career. By and large, however, researchers studying racial and ethnic minorities in STEM education have excluded these institutions, severely limiting the extent to which researchers, policymakers, and practitioners truly understand the ways they can increase success among this population in STEM education.

Fifth, we underscore the need for researchers to generate more informative and complex understandings of the ways in which STEM-specific support programs influence the experiences of racial and ethnic minority students. As we mentioned earlier in this volume, few programs have been evaluated using rigorous research methods. Thus, little knowledge exists regarding whether the broad range of programs that exist in K–12 schools and on college campuses are more effective or which STEM-specific support programs are more effective than others. Research is also needed on which components of existing programs are effective or futile. Museus (2010a) has offered one example of how researchers can examine targeted support programs to understand why they might work. Future research could employ similar approaches in the study of STEM-specific programs. Obviously, uncovering ineffective aspects of these programs is a much more sensitive and difficult task, particularly because programs are unlikely to reveal their weaknesses and risk future funding. Although researchers might not be able to completely avoid this issue, they can consider ways to protect the anonymity of programs and conduct qualitative analyses of both the strongest and weakest aspects of these programs.

Finally, it is important for researchers to continue to take stock of the literature on racial and ethnic minority students in STEM. Although our aim was to be as comprehensive as possible, such comprehensiveness can limit the ability to focus on specific subgroups in the racial and ethnic minority student population with greater depth. For example, a small and growing body of scholarship focused on this area suggests that minority women suffer from both gender and racial inequities in STEM education (see, for example, Chipman and Thomas, 1987; Huang, Taddese, Walter, and Peng, 2000; Johnson, 2007; Leslie, McClure, and Oaxaca, 1998; National Science Foundation, 2000a, 2000b; Oakes, 1990; Perna and others, 2009; Vining-Brown, 1994), so future analyses and syntheses of literature could focus on the experiences and outcomes of minority women in STEM. Another important area to understand is how socioeconomic status and race intersect to shape the experiences and outcomes of low-income minority students in the STEM circuit.

Implications for Future Policy

As we emphasize and reinforce throughout this volume, it is imperative that K–12 and higher education more effectively prepare and foster success among racial and ethnic minority students in the STEM education circuit. Accomplishing such a task on a broad scale requires policy based on empirical evidence and aimed at transforming the educational experience to cultivate greater levels of success among those students. This section provides five major implications for policy that is based on the preceding discussion and focused on increasing rates of success among racial and ethnic minorities in the STEM education circuit.

First, given the issues that we identified with academic tracking, K–12 school districts must enact policies that keep school personnel accountable for equitable placements of all students. Although we acknowledge that placing students in varying levels of mathematics courses might be inevitable, school districts should ensure that their personnel adopt assessments with the least bias possible. Furthermore, given that research indicates that racial and ethnic minorities are disproportionately tracked into low-ability classes, even when their scores on standardized assessments are equal to or better than those of their White peers (Flores, 2007; Oakes, 1995), K–12 educators should be required to engage in professional development and diversity training around how stereotyping—consciously or subconsciously—can affect their interactions with students and educational outcomes. Such training should encourage educators to hold high expectations for all students, even if they do not believe in their potential.

On a related note, federal and state policymakers should make efforts to ensure that all students have opportunities to enroll in Algebra I by eighth grade. Moreover, policymakers should consider the importance of funding programs that will help prepare all students to enroll in Algebra I by that point in their education. We see it as critical that students do not fall behind this early in their educational trajectory because of the likelihood that falling behind will lead to channeling into lower math tracks and greater challenges in high school and college.

Second, city and state leaders should recognize the important relationship between participating in Advanced Placement courses in high school and succeeding in the STEM circuit as well as the fact that many racial and ethnic minority students attend middle and high schools that do not offer Advanced Placement courses such as trigonometry and calculus (Adelman, 2006). Therefore, municipal and state leaders should ensure that schools serving large numbers of minority students, regardless of where they are located, have the necessary financial resources to offer such courses; not doing so deprives minority students of a quality education comparable to that of their counterparts who attend more affluent and predominantly White schools. Furthermore, city and state leaders must continue to make efforts to ensure that all students have access to highly qualified math and science teachers. In particular, they should consider providing additional incentives, especially debt forgiveness and generous salaries, to attract and keep such teachers at high-need schools.

Third, in addition to designing and enacting policies that draw larger numbers of highly qualified teachers, states should enact policies that ensure a more equitable distribution of funds across all school districts. More equity in funding systems would allow schools in low-income districts to secure more highly qualified teachers, up-to-date technology, and laboratories that could influence racial and ethnic minority students' interest in STEM. Securing these resources is critical to provide an academically intense curriculum for all students (Adelman, 2006). Such equal educational opportunities would allow schools to offer more Advanced Placement courses and enable high-achieving minority students in otherwise low-resource schools to reach their full potential and be prepared to excel in college-level mathematics and science courses.

Fourth, given the fact that AAPIs and Hispanics are the two fastest-growing racial groups in the United States, it is critical to concentrate on the unique challenges that generally disrupt their success. In particular, schools must implement bilingual education programs so AAPI and Hispanic students have the opportunity to master subject matter in more than one language. Federal policymakers could enact policies that provide incentives for schools to create or retain bilingual education programs. This form of intervention is necessary to strengthen educational opportunities inside the schools and create environments in which non-English-speaking AAPI and Hispanic students can become proficient in English and succeed.

Fifth, policymakers across all levels of government should be mindful that persistent problems in education are not just failed outcomes of educational policies and practices. Rather, disparities in education are complex and inextricably linked to other issues such as cultural conflict and insufficient income. For example, if many racial and ethnic minority students must enter, adjust to, and succeed in campus and STEM cultures that are very different from the cultures from which they come, policymakers should provide incentives for K–12 and college educators to employ innovative methods to engage the cultural backgrounds and communities of minority students in STEM, thereby making often alienating and disengaging curricula culturally relevant and engaging for diverse student populations.

With regard to income, many students struggle to pay for higher education, and such financial concerns are complex. Tuition continues to rise, and many undergraduates, particularly low-income minority students, choose to work full time while attending school full time; research shows that working more than twenty hours per week can be detrimental to retention and persistence (Pascarella and others, 1998). Recently, policymakers have failed to address these financial challenges adequately by placing greater emphases on loans instead of grants in the composition of financial aid packages. Moving forward, policymakers must work to provide more need-based gift aid allocations and ensure sufficient funding for programs that allow low-income racial and ethnic minority students to work on research projects in STEM departments for wages. Such opportunities will help prevent minority students from working too many hours in off-campus jobs that are unrelated to STEM fields, enhance their levels of engagement in STEM environments, and likely contribute to success. Considering these larger systemic issues by such methods acknowledges that societal context affects educational outcomes.

Implications for Future Practice

This section highlights five implications from our analysis and synthesis of the literature that might be helpful for educators serving racial and ethnic minority students in STEM education. First, educators should seek funding to create, expand, or build on the programs that have demonstrated effectiveness such as the interventions we described in the previous two chapters. These programs provide direct services that proactively address critical problems and provide positive opportunities and services, including cultivating collaborative and supportive educational environments, reinforcing students' self-efficacy, enhancing their problem-solving skills, teaching them research and technological skills, and providing opportunities for educationally purposeful interaction with faculty and peers.

Second, one of the most salient conclusions from our review of STEM programs and initiatives is that preliminary evidence suggests that two components of these programs might be particularly potent: (1) peer collaboration and community and (2) research experience in STEM. Schoolteachers and college faculty should avoid overrelying on independent learning opportunities and maximize the incorporation of peer community building in the classroom. As previously mentioned, when peer groups are formed and focused on STEM, they can integrate students' academic and social lives, increase their investment of energy in studying, and promote positive outcomes (Fullilove and Treisman, 1990; Treisman, 1992).

With regard to research experiences, college and university faculty should consider the importance of providing students with opportunities to be involved in undergraduate research. In ideal situations, funding can be used to pay students for their work on research projects. In cases in which such funding is not available to accommodate the pool of interested students, faculty should consider emphasizing that such opportunities can be created through independent studies. For example, faculty can teach group independent studies through which they can collaboratively design and conduct research with a team of undergraduate students. This implication may be difficult for any single faculty member to use because independent studies are often not counted toward annual faculty teaching loads. Some academic programs, however, have pushed or are pushing to implement policies that would allow group independent studies, with a certain number of students, to count toward faculty members' required teaching loads.

Third, in light of the previously mentioned research on the importance of collectivist cultures, teacher expectations, stereotype threat, and self-efficacy in racial and ethnic minority students' experiences and outcomes, schoolteachers and college faculty must create collective classroom cultures that value the success of all students, including racial and ethnic minorities, and send a message to those students that they can succeed in STEM. Indeed, individualistic cultures that thrive on competition may not have a positive impact on minority students who have been exposed to or bombarded with messages that they cannot be successful in STEM fields. Rather, evidence suggests that many of these students could benefit from instructors and classrooms that value collective pursuit of knowledge and an investment in the success of one another.

Fourth, as we mention throughout this volume, research has noted that many minority students do not believe that STEM courses are relevant to their backgrounds, lives, or academic and professional career trajectories (Clewell, Anderson, and Thorpe, 1992). Thus, although educators often assume that STEM course content cannot be culturally relevant, it is not necessarily the case. In fact, although review of such activity is beyond the scope of this monograph, faculty and students at some institutions have designed ways to incorporate racial and ethnic minority issues in STEM education curricula. Therefore, both K–12 and postsecondary educators should make conscious efforts to connect their STEM curricula to current issues in their students' ethnic communities. It might be in the form of service-learning activities that encourage minority students to identify and solve problems that exist in their home communities.

Last, educators should ensure that racial and ethnic minority students are exposed to STEM opportunities and careers early in and throughout the STEM education circuit. In addition, schools and college campuses should be intentional about hosting successful racial and ethnic minority STEM professionals as guest speakers. These speakers can serve as role models for minority students and, if they speak on topics that are culturally relevant, might help cultivate racial and ethnic minority students' passion for STEM subjects outside the classroom.

Conclusion

In sum, several important implications for future research, policy, and practice have emerged from this volume. The list offered herein is not exhaustive, but perhaps educators who read this volume will develop a more extensive set of implications to inform their efforts to increase success among racial and ethnic minority students in the STEM circuit. We urge researchers to think critically about ways to disaggregate their data and expand on areas of inquiry in which we lack sufficient evidence, call on policymakers to ensure the levels of funding that are necessary to support minority students who want to succeed in STEM, and implore all educators in the circuit to consider ways to make STEM education relevant to minority students' socioeconomic, cultural, racial, and geographic backgrounds.

This volume provides researchers, policymakers, and practitioners with a comprehensive analysis and synthesis of past research to help them understand the current knowledge base in this area so that they can use that information to take action toward increasing minority students' success in STEM. Indeed, now is a vital time to invest in all human potential to contribute to America's productivity and the increasingly global and knowledge-based economy. This volume is a call to action for all who are concerned about individual opportunity, the condition of our nation, and humankind to begin or continue investing in efforts to maximize success among all students in the STEM circuit toward the goals of expanding opportunity, reinforcing America's position as a leader in the global marketplace, and contributing to scientific and technological innovation that can improve lives for people around the world.

Notes

1. Throughout this monograph, we use "racial and ethnic minority" and "minority" interchangeably.
2. For the purposes of this monograph, we define the "STEM education circuit" or "STEM circuit" as a system of the multiple and varying educational pathways from science and math education in elementary school to completion of a terminal STEM degree (that is, the Ph.D.). Our discussion, however, focuses on the pathways in the circuit from elementary education to the completion of bachelor's degrees.

Appendix

The K-16 STEM Education Model

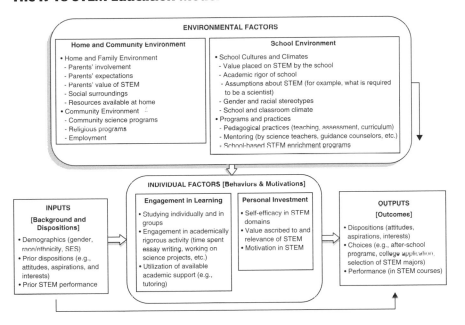

References

ACT, Inc. (2006). *Developing the STEM education pipeline.* Iowa City: ACT, Inc.

Adelman, C. (1999). *Answers in the tool box: Academic intensity, attendance patterns, and bachelor's degree attainment.* Washington, DC: Office of Educational Research and Improvement, U.S. Department of Education.

Adelman, C. (2006). *The toolbox revisited: Paths to degree completion from high school through college.* Washington, DC: U.S. Department of Education.

Agosto, D. E., Gasson, S., and Atwood, M. (2008). Changing mental models of the IT professions: A theoretical framework. *Journal of Information Technology Education, 7,* 205–221.

Ainsworth-Darnell, J. W., and Downey, D. B. (1998). Assessing the oppositional culture explanation for racial/ethnic differences in school performance. *American Sociological Review, 63*(4), 536–553.

Allen, W. R. (1992). The color of success: African-American college student outcomes at predominantly White and Historically Black public colleges and universities. *Harvard Educational Review, 62*(1), 26–44.

American Association for the Advancement of Science. (1989). *Science for all Americans.* New York: American Association for the Advancement of Science.

American Council on Education. (2006). *Increasing the success of minority students in science and technology.* Washington, DC: American Council on Education.

Ancis, J. R., Sedlacek, W. E., and Mohr, J. J. (2000). Student perceptions of campus cultural climate by race. *Journal of Counseling and Development, 78,* 180–185.

Anderson, B. J. (1990). Minorities and mathematics: The new frontier and challenge of the nineties. *Journal of Negro Education, 59*(3), 260–272.

Anderson, B. J. (1996). Strengthening mathematics education: Critical skills for the new majority. In L. Rendon and R. Hope (Eds.), *Educating a new majority* (pp. 201–218). San Francisco: Jossey-Bass.

Anderson, E., and Kim, D. (2006). *Increasing the success of minority students in science and technology.* Washington, DC: American Council on Education.

Arbona, C., and Novy, D. M. (1990). Noncognitive dimensions as predictors of college success among Black, Mexican-American, and White students. *Journal of College Student Development, 31,* 415–422.

Aronson, J., and others. (1999). When White men can't do math: Necessary and sufficient factors in stereotype threat. *Journal of Experimental Social Psychology, 35,* 29–46.

Aronson, J., Fried, C. B., and Good, C. (2002). Reducing the effects of stereotype threat on African American college students by shaping theories of intelligence. *Journal of Experimental Social Psychology, 38,* 113–125.

Aronson, J., Quinn, D. M., and Spencer, S. J. (1998). Stereotype threat and the academic underperformance of minorities and women. In J. K. Swim and C. Stangor (Eds.), *Prejudice: The target's perspective* (pp. 83–103). San Diego: Academic Press.

Astin, A. M. (1982). *Minorities in American higher education: Recent trends, current prospects, and recommendations.* San Francisco: Jossey-Bass.

Astin, A. W. (1993). *What matters in college? Four critical years revisited.* San Francisco: Jossey-Bass.

Astin, A. W., and Astin, H. S. (1992). *Undergraduate science education: The impact of different college environments on the educational pipeline in the sciences.* Final Report. Los Angeles: Higher Education Research Institute.

Babco, E. L. (2003). *Trends in African American and Native American participation in STEM higher education.* New York: Commission on Professionals in Science and Technology.

Babco, E. L. (2005). *The status of Native Americans in science and engineering.* Washington, DC: Commission on Professionals in Science and Technology.

Baird, L. L. (2000). College climate and the Tinto model. In J. M. Braxton (Ed.), *Reworking the student departure puzzle* (pp. 62–80). Nashville: Vanderbilt University Press.

Bandura, A. (1977). Self-efficacy: Toward a unifying theory of behavioral change. *Psychological Review, 84*(2), 191–215.

Bandura, A. (1997). *Self-efficacy: The exercise of control.* New York: W. H. Freeman.

Barlow, A.E.L., and Villarejo, M. (2004). Making a difference for minorities: Evaluation of an educational enrichment program. *Journal of Research in Science Teaching, 41*(9), 861–881.

Barnhardt, R., and Kawagley, A. O. (2005). Indigenous knowledge systems and Alaska Native ways of knowing. *Anthropology and Education Quarterly, 36*(1), 8–23.

Bauer, K. W. (1998). Editor's notes. *New Directions for Institutional Research* (No. 98, pp. 1–5). San Francisco: Jossey-Bass.

Baum, S., and Payea, K. (2005). *Education pays, 2004: The benefits of higher education for individuals and society.* New York: College Board.

Beane, D. B. (1990). Say Yes to a youngster's future: A model for home, school, and community partnership. *Journal of Negro Education, 59*(3), 360–374.

Becker, G. (1964). *Human capital: A theoretical and empirical analysis, with special reference to education.* New York: National Bureau of Economic Research.

Bell, D. A. (1987). *And we are not saved: The elusive quest for racial justice.* New York: Basic Books.

Bennett, C., McWhorter, L., and Kuykendall, J. (2006). Will I ever teach? Latino and African American students' perspectives on PRAXIS I. *American Educational Research Journal, 43*(3), 531–574.

Berryman, S. E. (1983). *Who will do science?* New York: Rockefeller Foundation.

Bissell, J. (2000). Changing the face of science and engineering: Good beginnings for the twenty-first century. In G. Campbell, Jr., R. Denes, and C. Morrison (Eds.), *Access denied: Race, ethnicity, and scientific enterprise* (pp. 61–77). New York: Oxford University Press.

Bonous-Hammarth, M. (2000). Pathways to success: Affirming opportunities for science, mathematics, and engineering majors. *Journal of Negro Education, 69*(1–2), 92–111.

Bonous-Hammarth, M. (2006). Promoting student participation in science, technology, engineering and mathematics careers. In W. R. Allen, M. Bonous-Hammarth, and R. T. Teranishi (Eds.), *Higher education in a global society: Achieving diversity, equity, and excellence* (pp. 269 282). Oxford: Elsevier.

Borden, V.M.H., and Brown, P. C. (2004). The top 100: Interpreting the data. *Black Issues in Higher Education, 21*(8), 3.

Bowen, W. G., and Bok, D. (1998). *The shape of the river: Long-term consequences of considering race in college and university admissions.* Princeton, NJ: Princeton University Press.

Branch-Brioso, K. (2009). What will it take to increase Hispanics in STEM? Money, of course. *Diverse Education.* Retrieved December 16, 2010, from http://diverseeducation.com/cache/print.php?articleId=12347.

Brand, B. R., Glasson, G. E., and Green, A. M. (2006). Sociocultural issues influencing students' learning in science and mathematics: An analysis of the perspectives of African American students. *School Science and Mathematics, 106*(5), 228–236.

Braxton, J. M. (2000). Introduction. In J. M. Braxton (Ed.), *Reworking the student departure puzzle* (pp. 1–8). Nashville: Vanderbilt University Press.

Braxton, J. M., Sullivan, A. S., and Johnson, R. M. (1997). Appraising Tinto's theory of college student departure. In J. C. Smart (Ed.), *Higher education: A handbook of theory and research* (Vol. 12, pp. 107–164). New York: Agathon Press.

Breland, H., and others. (2002). *Trends in college admission 2000: A report of a national survey of undergraduate admission policies, practices, and procedures.* Alexandria, VA: National Association for College Admission Counseling.

Brown, B. (2004). Discursive identity: Assimilation into the culture of science and its implications for minority students. *Journal of Research in Science Teaching, 41*(8), 810–834.

Brown, C. M., II. (1999). Ebony men in the ivory tower: A policy perspective. In V. C. Polite and J. E. Davis (Eds.), *African American males in school and society: Practices and policies for effective education* (pp. 122–133). New York: Teachers College Press.

Brown, I., Jr., and Inouye, D. K. (1978). Learned helplessness through modeling: The role of perceived similarity in competence. *Journal of Personality and Social Psychology, 36,* 900–908.

Brown, S. W. (2002). Hispanic students majoring in science or engineering: What happened in their educational journeys? *Journal of Women and Minorities in Science and Engineering, 8,* 123–148.

Burn, H., and Holloway, J. (2006). *Why should I care? Student motivation in an introductory programming course.* Proceedings of the ASEE Annual Conference and Exposition, Chicago, IL.

Business–Higher Education Forum. (2005). *A commitment to America's future: Responding to the crisis in mathematics and science education.* Washington, DC: Business–Higher Education Forum.

Cabrera, A., and others. (1999). Campus racial climate and the adjustment of students to college: A comparison between White students and African-American students. *Journal of Higher Education, 70,* 134–160.

Cabrera, A. F., and others. (2002). Collaborative learning: Its impact on college students' development and diversity. *Journal of College Student Development, 43,* 20–34.

Cabrera, A. F., Colbeck C. L., and Terenzini, P. T. (2001). Developing performance indicators for assessing classroom teaching practices and student learning: The case of engineering. *Research in Higher Education, 42,* 327–352.

Cabrera, A. F., Nora, A., and Castañeda, M. B. (1992). The role of finances in the persistence process: A structural model. *Research in Higher Education 33*(5), 571–593.

Cabrera, A. F., Stampen, J. O., and Hansen, W. L. (1990). Exploring the effects of ability to pay on persistence in college. *Review of Higher Education, 13*(3), 303–336.

Carnevale, A. P., and Desrochers, D. M. (2003). Preparing students for the knowledge economy: What school counselors need to know. *Professional School Counseling, 6*(4), 228–236.

Ceja, B. D., and Rhodes, J. H. (2004). Through the pipeline: The role of faculty in promoting associate degree completion among Hispanic students. *Community College Journal of Research and Practice, 28*(3), 249–262.

Chang, J. C. (2002). *Women and minorities in the science, mathematics and engineering pipeline.* Los Angeles: ERIC Clearinghouse for Community Colleges.

Chang, M. J. (2007). Beyond artificial integration: Re-imagining cross-racial interactions among undergraduates. In S. R. Harper and S. Hurtado (Eds.), *Responding to the realities of race on campus.* New Directions for Student Services (No. 120, pp. 25–38).

Chang, M. J., Cerna, O., Han, J., and Sàenz, V. (2008). The contradictory roles of institutional status in retaining underrepresented minorities in biomedical and behavioral science majors. *Review of Higher Education, 31*(4), 433–464.

Chapa, J., and De La Rosa, B. (2006). The problematic pipeline: Demographic trends and Latino participation in graduate science, technology, engineering, and mathematics programs. *Journal of Hispanic Higher Education, 5*(3), 203–221.

Chen, T. T., and Farr, J. L. (2007). An empirical test of the glass ceiling effect for Asian Americans in science and engineering. In R. Burke and M. Mattis (Eds.), *Women and minorities in science, technology, engineering, and mathematics* (pp. 128–156). Cheltenham, UK: Edward Elgar.

Child Trends Databank. (2005). *Dropout rates.* Retrieved October 27, 2010, from http://www.childtrendsdatabank.org/pdf/1_PDF.pdf.

Chipman, S. F., and Thomas, V. G. (1987). The participation of women and minorities in mathematical, scientific, and technical fields. *Review of Research in Education, 14*(1), 387–430.

Chou, R. S., and Feagin, J. R. (2008). *The myth of the model minority: Asian Americans facing racism.* Boulder, CO: Paradigm.

Choy, S., and Li, X. (2005). *Debt burden: A comparison of 1992–93 and 1999–2000 bachelor's degree recipients a year after graduating* (NCES 2005-170). U.S. Department of Education. Washington, DC: National Center for Education Statistics.

Choy, S. P. (1999). College access and affordability. *Education Statistics Quarterly, 1*(2), 74–90.

Choy, S. P. (2004). Paying for college: Changes between 1990 and 2000 for full-time dependent undergraduates. In *Condition of Education 2004.* Washington, DC: National Center for Education Statistics.

Clewell, B. C., Anderson, B. T., and Thorpe, M. E. (1992). *Breaking the barriers: Helping female and minority students succeed in mathematics and science.* San Francisco: Jossey-Bass.

Cofer, J. (2000). A comparison of the influence of debtload on the persistence of students at public and private colleges. *Journal of Student Financial Aid, 30*(2), 30–58.

Cofer, J., and Somers, P. (2000). Within-year persistence of students at two-year colleges. *Community College Journal of Research and Practice, 24,* 785–807.

Cohen, L. L., and Swim, J. K. (1995). The differential impact of gender ratios on women and men: Tokenism, self-confidence, and expectations. *Personality and Social Psychology Bulletin, 21,* 876–884.

Colbeck, C. L., Cabrera, A. F., and Terenzini, P. T. (2001). Leaning professional confidence: Linking teaching practices, students' self-perceptions, and gender. *Review of Higher Education, 24*(2), 173–191.

Cole, D., and Espinoza, A. (2008). Examining the academic success of Latino students in science, technology, engineering, and mathematics (STEM) majors. *Journal of College Student Development, 49*(4), 285–300.

Cole, S., and Barber, E. (2003). *Increasing faculty diversity: The occupational choices of high-achieving minority students.* Cambridge, MA: Harvard University Press.

College Board. (2008). *Facts, not fiction: Setting the record straight.* New York: College Board.

College Board. (2010). *What it costs to go to college.* New York: College Board.

Collins, M. (1992). *Ordinary children, extraordinary teachers.* Charlottesville, VA: Hampton Roads Publishing Company.

Committee on Prospering in the Global Economy of the 21st Century. (2007). *Rising above the gathering storm: Energizing and employing America for a brighter economic future.* Washington, DC: National Academies Press.

Contreras, F., Bensimon, E., and Malcom, L. (2008). An equity-based accountability framework for Hispanic-serving institutions. In M. Gasman, B. Baez, and C. Turner, *Interdisciplinary approaches to understanding minority-serving institutions* (pp. 71–90). Albany, NY: SUNY Press.

Cook, P. J., and Ludwig, J. (1998). The burden of "acting white": Do Black adolescents disparage academic achievement? In C. Jencks and M. Phillips (Eds.), *The Black White test score gap* (pp. 375–400). Washington, DC: Brookings Institution Press.

Cote, J. E., and Levin, C. (1997). Students' motivations, learning environments, and human capital acquisitions: Toward an integrated paradigm of student development. *Journal of College Student Development, 38*(3), 229–243.

Crenshaw, K., Gotanda, N., Peller, G., and Thomas, K. (1995). Introduction. In K. Crenshaw, N. Gotanda, G. Peller, and K. Thomas (Eds.), *Critical race theory: The key writings that formed the movement* (pp. xii–xxxii). New York: New Press.

Cress, C. M., and Ikeda, E. K. (2003). Distress under duress: The relationship between campus climate and depression in Asian American college students. *NASPA Journal, 40*(2), 74–97.

Croizet, J., and Claire, T. (1998). Extending the concept of stereotype and threat to social class: The intellectual underperformance of students from low socioeconomic backgrounds. *Personality and Social Psychology Bulletin, 24*(6), 588–594.

Cross, S. E., and Vick, N. V. (2001). The interdependent self-construal and social support: The case of persistence in engineering. *Personality and Social Psychology Bulletin, 27,* 820–832.

Cullinane, J., and Leegwater, L. (2009). *Diversifying the STEM pipeline: The Model Replication Institutions Program.* Washington, DC: Institute for Higher Education Policy.

Darling-Hammond, L. (2000). Teacher quality and student achievement: A review of state policy evidence. *Educational Policy Analysis Archives, 8*(1). Retrieved December 16, 2010, from http://epaa.asu.edu/epaa/v8n1/.

Davis, C. G., and Finelli, C. J. (2007). Diversity and retention in engineering. In M. Kaplan and A. T. Miller (Eds.), *Scholarship of multicultural teaching and learning.* New Directions for Teaching and Learning (No. 111, pp. 63–71). San Francisco: Jossey-Bass.

Davis, J. E. (1994). College in Black and White: Campus environments and academic achievement of African American males. *Journal of Negro Education, 63*(4), 620–633.

De La Cruz, Y. (1998). Issues in teaching math and science to Latinos. In M. L. Gonzalez., A. Huerta-Macias, and J. V. Tinajero (Eds.), *Educating Latino students: A guide to successful practice* (pp. 161–175). Lancaster, PA: Technomic Publishing Company.

Delgado, R., and Stefancic, J. (2001). *Critical race theory: An introduction.* New York: New York University Press.

Denson, C. D., Avery, Z. A., and Schell, J. D. (2010). Critical inquiry into urban African-American students' perceptions of engineering. *Journal of African American Studies, 14*(1), 61–74.

Denson, N., and Chang, M. J. (2009). Racial diversity matters: The impact of diversity-related student engagement and institutional context. *American Educational Research Journal, 46*(2), 322–353.

DesJardins, S. L., Ahlburg, D. A., and McCall, B. P. (2002). A temporal investigation of factors related to timely degree completion. *Journal of Higher Education, 73*(5), 555–581.

Dixson, A. D., and Rousseau, C. K. (2006). *Critical race theory in education: All God's children got a song.* New York: Routledge.

Dowd, A. C., and Coury, T. (2006). The effects of loans on persistence and attainment of community college students. *Research in Higher Education, 47*(1), 33–62.

Dowd, A. C., Malcom, L. E., and Bensimon, E. M. (2009). Benchmarking the success of Latina and Latino students in STEM to achieve national graduation goals. Los Angeles: University of Southern California.

Drew, D. (1996). *Aptitude revisited: Rethinking math and science education for America's next century.* Baltimore: Johns Hopkins University Press.

Duderstadt, J. J. (1990). America at the crossroads: The challenge of science education. In W. R. Wineke and P. Certain (Eds.), *The freshman year in science and engineering: Old problems, new perspectives for research universities* (pp. 21–27). University Park, PA: Alliance for Undergraduate Education.

Ehrenberg, R. (1991). The demographic distribution of American doctorates. In C. Clotfelter, R. Ehrenberg, M. Getz, and J. Siegfried (Eds.), *Economic challenges in higher education* (pp. 211–232). Chicago: University of Chicago Press.

Eimers, M., and Pike, G. (1997). Minority and nonminority adjustment to college: Differences or similarities? *Research in Higher Education, 38,* 77–97.

Elliott, R., and others. (1996). The role of ethnicity in choosing and leaving science in highly selective institutions. *Research in Higher Education, 37*(6), 681–709.

Farkas, G., Lleras, C., and Maczuga, S. (2002). Does oppositional culture exist in minority and poverty peer groups? *American Sociological Review 67*(1), 148–155.

Farrell, E. F. (2002). Engineering a warmer welcome for female students. *Chronicle of Higher Education, 48,* A31.

Feagin, J. R., Vera, H., and Imani, N. (1996). *The agony of education: Black students at White colleges and universities.* New York: Routledge.

Fenske, R. H., Porter, J. D., and DuBrock, C. P. (2000). Tracking financial aid and persistence of women, minority, and needy students in science, engineering, and mathematics. *Research in Higher Education, 41*(1), 67–94.

Fergus, E. (2009). Understanding Latino students' schooling experiences: The relevance of skin color among Mexican and Puerto Rican high school students. *Teachers College Record, 111*(2), 339–375.

Fisk, A. P., Kitayama, S., Markus, H. R., and Nisbett, R. E. (1998). The cultural matrix of social psychology. In D. Gilbert, S. Fiske, and G. Lindzey (Eds.), *Handbook of social psychology* (4th ed., Vol. 2, pp. 915–981). Boston: McGraw-Hill.

Fleming, J. (1984). *Blacks in college: A comparative study of students' success in Black and White institutions.* San Francisco: Jossey-Bass.

Fleming, J. (2000). Knocking at freedom's door: Race, equity, and affirmative action in U.S. higher education. *Journal of Negro Education, 69*(1/2), 27–37.

Fleming, J. (2002). Who will succeed in college? When SAT predicts Black students' performance. *Review of Higher Education, 25*(3), 281–296.

Fleming, J., and Garcia, N. (1998). Are standardized tests fair to African Americans? Predictive validity of the SAT in Black and White institutions. *Journal of Higher Education, 69*(5), 471–495.

Flores, A. (2007). Examining disparities in mathematics education: Achievement gap or opportunity gap? *High School Journal, 91*(1), 29–42.

Ford, D. Y., Grantham, T. G., and Whiting, G. W. (2008). Another look at the achievement gap: Learning from the experiences of gifted Black students. *Urban Education, 43*(2), 216–239.

Ford, M. E. (1992). *Motivating humans: Goals, emotions, and personal agency beliefs.* San Francisco: Sage.

Fordham, S., and Ogbu, J. (1986). Black students' school success: Coping with the burden of acting White. *Urban Review, 18*(3), 176–206.

Fries-Britt, S., and Turner, B. (2001). Facing stereotypes: A case study of Black students on a White campus. *Journal of College Student Development, 42,* 420–429.

Fries-Britt, S., and Turner, B. (2002). Uneven stories: Successful Black collegians at a Black and a White campus. *Review of Higher Education, 25*(3), 315–330.

Fries-Britt, S., Younger, T., and Hall, W. (2010). How perceptions of race and campus racial climate impact underrepresented minorities in physics. In T. E. Dancy II (Ed.), *Managing diversity: (Re)visioning equity on college campuses* (pp. 181–198). New York: Peter Lang.

Fries-Britt, S., Younger, T., and Hall, W. (2010). Lessons from high achieving minorities in physics. In S. R. Harper, C. Newman, and S. Gary (Eds.), *Students of color in STEM: Constructing a new research agenda.* New Directions for Institutional Research No. 148, 75–83. San Francisco: Jossey-Bass.

Fullilove, R. E., and Treisman, E. M. (1990). Mathematics achievement among African American undergraduates at the University of California, Berkeley: An evaluation of the mathematics workshop program. *Journal of Negro Education, 59*(3), 463–478.

Gainen, J. (1995). Barriers to success in quantitative gateway courses. In J. Gainen and E. Willemsen (Eds.), *Fostering success in quantitative gateway courses.* San Francisco: Jossey-Bass.

Gamoran, A., Porter, A. C., Smithson, J., and White, P. A. (1997). Upgrading high school mathematics instruction: Improving learning opportunities for low-achieving, low-income youth. *American Evaluation and Policy Analysis, 19*(4), 325–338.

Gándara, P. (2006). Strengthening the academic pipeline leading to careers in math, science, and technology for Latino students. *Journal of Hispanic Higher Education, 5*(3), 222–237.

Gándara, P., and Contreras, F. (2009). *The Latino education crisis: The consequences of failed social policies.* Cambridge, MA: Harvard University Press.

Gándara, P., and Maxwell-Jolly, J. (1999). *Priming the pump: Strategies for increasing underrepresented minority graduates.* New York: College Board.

Garrison, H. H. (1987). Undergraduate science and engineering education for Black and Native Americans. In L. S. Dix (Ed.), *Minorities: Their underrepresentation and career differentials in science and engineering.* Proceedings of a workshop. Washington, DC: National Academy Press.

General Accounting Office. (1995). *Higher education: Restructuring student aid could reduce low-income student dropout rate.* (GAO/HEHS-95-48). Washington, DC: U.S. Government Printing Office.

Georges, A. (1999). Keeping what we've got: Effective strategies for retaining minority freshmen in engineering. *NACME Research Letter, 9,* 1–19.

Gerardi, S. (2005). Self-concept of ability as a predictor of academic success among urban technical college students. *Social Science Journal, 42,* 295–300.

Glater, J. D. (2006, March 14). Colleges open minority aid to all comers. *New York Times*. Retrieved December 16, 2010, from http://www.nytimes.com/2006/03/14/education/14minority.htm1?.

Glennen, R. E., and Baxley, D. M. (1985). Reduction of attrition through intrusive advising. *NASPA Journal, 22*, 10–14.

Gloria, A. M., Castellanos, J., Lopez, A. G., and Rosales, R. (2005). An examination of the academic nonpersistence decisions of Latino undergraduates. *Hispanic Journal of Behavioral Sciences, 27*(2), 202–223.

Gloria, A. M., and Kurpius, S.E.R. (2001). Influences of self-beliefs, social support, and comfort in the university environment on the academic nonpersistence decisions of American Indian undergraduates. *Cultural Diversity and Ethnic Minority Psychology, 7*(1), 88–102.

Goel, J. (2006). An invisible minority: Asian Americans in mathematics. *Notices of the American Mathematical Society, 53*(8), 878–882.

Goldhaber, D. D., and Brewer, D. J. (1997a). Evaluating the effects of teacher degree level on educational performance. In W. J. Fowler (Ed.), *Developments in school finance, 1996* (pp. 192–210). Washington, DC: National Center for Education Statistics, U.S. Department of Education.

Goldhaber, D. D., and Brewer, D. J. (1997b).Why don't schools and teachers seem to matter? Assessing the impact of unobservable on educational productivity. *Journal of Human Resources, 32*(3), 505–523.

Goldhaber, D. D., and Brewer, D. J. (2000). Does teacher certification matter? High school teacher certification status and student achievement. *Educational Evaluation and Policy Analysis, 22*(2), 129–145.

Gonzalez, K. P. (2003). Campus culture and the experiences of Chicano students in a predominantly White university. *Urban Education, 37*(2), 193–218.

Good, C., Aronson, J., and Harder, J. A. (1999). *Stereotype threat in the absence of a kernel of truth: Women in calculus.* Unpublished manuscript. Austin: University of Texas.

Good, C., Aronson, J., and Inzlicht, M. (2003). Improving adolescents' standardized test performance: An intervention to reduce the effects of stereotype threat. *Journal of Applied Developmental Psychology, 24*, 645–662.

Good, J. M., Halpin, G., and Halpin, G. (2002a). Retaining Black students in engineering: Do minority programs have a longitudinal impact? *Journal of College Student Retention, 3*(4), 351–364.

Good, J. M., Halpin, G., and Halpin, G. (2002b). Enhancing and evaluating mathematical and scientific problem-solving skills of African American college freshmen. *Equity & Excellence in Education, 35*(1), 50–58.

Grandy, J. (1994). *Gender and ethnic differences among science and engineering majors: Experiences, achievements, and expectations.* Princeton, NJ: Educational Testing Service.

Grandy, J. (1998). Persistence in science of high-ability minority students. *Journal of Higher Education, 69*(6), 589–620.

Grant, C. A. (2004). Oppression, privilege, and high-stakes testing. *Multicultural perspectives, 6*, 3–11.

Green, A., and Glasson, G. (2009). African Americans majoring in science at predominantly White universities: A review of literature. *College Student Journal, 43,* 366–374.

Green, R. (1978). Math avoidance: A barrier to American Indian science education and science careers. *Bureau of Indian Affairs Education Research Bulletin, 6*(3), 1–8. ERIC Document Reproduction Service ED 170 084.

Gregerman, S. R. (1999). Improving the academic success of diverse students through undergraduate research. *Council on Undergraduate Research Quarterly, 20*(2), 54–59.

Guiffrida, D. A. (2003). African American student organizations as agents of social integration. *Journal of College Student Development, 44*(3), 304–319.

Guiffrida, D. A. (2006). Toward a cultural advancement of Tinto's theory. *Review of Higher Education, 29*(4), 451–472.

Gutstein, E., Lipman, P., Hernandez, P., and de los Reyes, R. (1997). Culturally relevant mathematics teaching in a Mexican American context. *Journal of Research in Mathematics Education, 28*(6), 709–737.

Hackett, G., Betz, N. E., Casas, J., and Rocha-Singh, I. A. (1992). Gender, ethnicity, and social cognitive factors predicting the academic achievement of students in engineering. *Journal of Counseling Psychology, 3*(4), 527–538.

Hall, E. R., and Post-Kammer, P. (1987). Black mathematics and science majors: Why so few? *Career Development Quarterly, 35*(3), 206–219.

Hall-Greene, D. (2000). A qualitative study on African American and Caribbean Black males' experience in a college of aeronautical science. Unpublished doctoral dissertation, Virginia Tech.

Haney, C., and Hurtado, A. (1994). The jurisprudence of race and meritocracy: Standardized testing and "race-neutral" racism in the workplace. *Law and Human Behavior, 18*(3), 223–248.

Hanson, S. L. (2004). African American women in science: Experiences from high school through the postsecondary years and beyond. *NWSA Journal, 16*(1), 96–115.

Harper, S. R., and Hurtado, S. (2007). Nine themes in campus racial climates. In S. R. Harper and L. D. Patton (Eds.), *Responding to the realities of race on campus.* New Directions for Student Services (pp. 7–24). San Francisco: Jossey-Bass.

Harper, S. R., Patton, L. D., and Wooden, O. S. (2009). Access and equity for African American students in higher education: A critical race historical analysis of policy efforts. *Journal of Higher Education, 80*(4), 389–414.

Harper, S. R., and Quaye, S. J. (2007). Student organizations as venues for Black identity expression and development among African American male student leaders. *Journal of College Student Development, 48*(2), 127–144.

Hathaway, R. S. (2003). UROP engineering retention analyses: UROP and non-UROP engineering retention comparison. Unpublished report, University of Michigan.

Hathaway, R. S., Nagda, B. A., and Gregerman, S. R. (2002). The relationship of undergraduate research participation to graduate and professional educational pursuit: An empirical study. *Journal of College Student Development, 43*(5), 614–631.

Heller, D. E. (2003). *Informing public policy: Financial aid and student persistence.* Boulder, CO: Western Interstate Commission for Higher Education.

Helms, J. E. (1994). The conceptualization of racial identity and other racial constructs. In E. J. Trickett, R. J. Watts, and D. Birman (Eds.), *Human diversity: Perspectives on people in context* (pp. 285–311). San Francisco: Jossey-Bass.

Hernandez, J. C. (2000). Understanding the retention of Latino college students. *Journal of College Student Development, 41*(6) 575–586.

Hernandez, J. C., and Lopez, M. A. (2004–05). Leaking pipeline: Issues impacting Latino/a college student retention. *Journal of College Student Retention, 6*(1), 37–60.

Higher Education Research Institute. (2010). *Degrees of success: Bachelor's degree completion rates among initial STEM majors.* Los Angeles: Higher Education Research Institute.

Hill, H. C., Rowan, B., and Ball, D. L. (2005). Effects of teachers' mathematical knowledge for teaching on student achievement. *American Educational Research Journal, 42*(2), 371–406.

Hill, K. (1990). The Detroit Area Pre-College Engineering Program, Inc. (DAPCEP). *Journal of Negro Education, 59*(3), 439–448.

Hilton, T. L., Hsia, J., Solórzano, D. G., and Benton, N. L. (1989). *Persistence in science of high ability minority students.* National Science Foundation Grant No. MDR-8652096. Princeton, NJ: Educational Testing Service.

Holt, J. K. (2006). An evaluation of math and science educational and occupational persistence among minorities. Proceedings from the 2006 annual meeting of the Eastern Education Research Association, Hilton Head, SC.

Horn, C. L., and Flores, S. M. (2003). The percentage plan in college admissions: A comparative analysis of the three states' experiences. Cambridge: MA: The Civil Rights Project at Harvard University. Retrieved December 16, 2010, from http://civilrightsprojects .harvard.edu/research.affirmativeaction/tristate.pdf.

Howard, J., and Hammond, R. (1985). Rumors of inferiority: The hidden obstacles of Black success. *New Republic, 9,* 17–21.

Hrabowski, F. A. (2003). Raising minority achievement in science and math. *Educational Leadership, 60*(4), 44–48.

Hrabowski, F. A., and Maton, K. I. (1995). Enhancing the success of African American students in the sciences: Freshman year outcomes. *School of Science and Mathematics, 95*(1), 19–27.

Hrabowski, F. A., and Maton, K. I. (2009). Change institutional culture, and you change who goes into science. *Academic, 95*(3), 11–16.

Huang, G., Taddese, N., Walter, E., and Peng, S. S. (2000). *Entry and persistence of women and minorities in college science and engineering education.* Washington, DC: National Center for Education Statistics.

Hune, S. (2002). Demographics and diversity of Asian American college students. In M. K. McEwen and others (Eds.), *Working with Asian American college students.* New Directions for Student Services (No. 97, pp. 11–20). San Francisco: Jossey-Bass.

Hurtado, S. (1992). The campus racial climate: Contexts and conflict. *Journal of Higher Education, 63*(5), 539–567.

Hurtado, S., and others. (2007). Predicting transition and adjustment to college: Biomedical and behavioral science aspirants' and minority students' first year of college. *Research in Higher Education, 48*(7), 481–887.

Hurtado, S., and others. (2008). Training future scientists: Predicting first-year minority student participation in health science research. *Research in Higher Education, 49*(2), 126–152.

Hurtado, S., and others. (2009). Diversifying science: Underrepresented student experiences in structured research programs. *Research in Higher Education, 50*(2), 189–214.

Hurtado, S., and Carter, D. (1997). Effects of college transition and perceptions of the campus racial climate on Latina/o college students' sense of belonging. *Sociology of Education, 70,* 324–345.

Hurtado, S., Carter, D., and Spuler, A. (1996). Latina/o student transition to college: Assessing difficulties and factors in successful college adjustment. *Research in Higher Education, 37,* 135–157.

Institute for Higher Education Policy. (2001). *Getting through college: Voices of low-income and minority students in New England.* Washington, DC: Institute for Higher Education Policy.

Institute for Higher Education Policy. (2009). *Diversifying the STEM pipeline: The model replication institutions program.* Washington, DC: Institute for Higher Education Policy.

Inzlicht, M., and Ben-Zeev, T. (2000). A threatening intellectual environment: Why females are susceptible to experiencing problem-solving deficits in the presence of males. *Psychological Science, 11,* 365–371.

Jackson, A. P., Smith, S. A., and Hill, C. L. (2003). Academic persistence among Native American college students. *Journal of College Student Development, 44*(4), 548–565.

Jackson, L. A., Gardner, P. D., and Sullivan, L. A. (1993). Engineering persistence: Past, present, and future factors and gender differences. *Higher Education, 26*(2), 227–246.

James, K. (2000). Social psychology: American Indians, science, and technology. *Social Science Computer Review, 18*(2), 196–213.

Jarosz, J. (2003). Engineering for Native Americans. *Winds of change: A magazine for American Indians in science and technology, 18*(3), 52–57.

JBHE Foundation. (2005–06). The growing list of colleges that have rejected the use of the SAT. *Journal of Blacks in Higher Education, 50,* 45–46.

Jencks, C., and Phillips, M. (1998). The black-white test score gap: An introduction. In C. Jencks and M. Phillips (Eds.), *The black-white test score gap* (pp. 1–55). Washington, DC: Brookings Institution Press.

Johnson, A. C. (2007). Unintended consequences: How science professors discourage women of color. *Science Education, 91*(5), 805–821.

Kaltenbaugh, L. S., St. John, E. P., and Starkey, J. B. (1999). What differences does tuition make? An analysis of ethnic differences in persistence. *Journal of Student Financial Aid, 29*(2), 21–31.

Kane, M. A., Beals, C., Valeau, E. J., and Johnson, M. J. (2004). Fostering success among traditionally underrepresented student groups: Hartnell College's approach to implementation of the math, engineering, and science achievement (MESA) program. *Community College Journal of Research and Practice, 28,* 17–26.

Kane, T. J. (1998). Misconceptions in the debate over affirmative action in college admissions. In G. Orfield and E. Miller (Eds.), *Chilling admissions: The affirmative action crisis and the search for alternatives* (pp. 17–31). Cambridge, MA: Harvard Education Publishing Group.

Kanter, R. M. (1977). *Men and women of the corporation.* New York: Basic Books.

Kao, G., and Tienda, M. (1998). Educational aspirations of minority youth. *American Journal of Education, 106,* 349–384.

Kaomea, J. (2003). Reading erasures and making the familiar strange: Defamiliarizing methods for research in formerly colonized and historically oppressed communities. *Educational Researcher, 32*(2), 14–25.

Kelly, P. J. (2005). *As America becomes more diverse: The impact of state higher education inequality.* Boulder, CO: National Center for Higher Education Management Systems.

Kiang, P. (1997). Pedagogies of life and death: Transforming immigrant/refugee students and Asian American studies. *Positions, 5*(2), 551–577.

Kiang, P. (2002). Stories and structures of persistence: Ethnographic learning through research and practice in Asian American studies. In Y. Zou and H. T. Trueba (Eds.), *Advances in Ethnographic research: From our theoretical and methodological roots to postmodern critical ethnography.* Lanham, MD: Rowman & Littlefield.

Kiehl, R. (1971). Opportunities for Blacks in engineering: A third report. *Personnel and Guidance Journal, 50*(3), 204–208.

Kim, M. K., and Conrad, C. (2006). The impact of historically Black colleges and universities on the academic success of African-American students. *Research in Higher Education, 47*(4), 399–427.

Kuh, G. D. (2005). Getting off the dime. In *Exploring different dimensions of student engagement: 2005 annual report.* Bloomington, IN: Center for Postsecondary Research.

Kuh, G. D., and others. (2007). Piecing together the student success puzzle: Research, propositions, and recommendations. ASHE-ERIC Higher Education Report, 32(5). San Francisco: Jossey-Bass.

Kuh, G. D., and Love, P. G. (2000). A cultural perspective on student departure. In J. M. Braxton (Ed.), *Reworking the student departure puzzle* (pp. 196–212). Nashville: Vanderbilt University Press.

Kuh, G. D., and Whitt, E. J. (1988). *The invisible tapestry: Culture in American colleges and universities.* ASHE-ERIC Higher Education Report, No. 1. Washington, DC: Association for the Study of Higher Education.

Ladson-Billings, G. (1995a). But that's just good teaching! The case for culturally relevant pedagogy. *Theory into Practice, 34*(3), 159–165.

Ladson-Billings, G. (1995b). Toward a theory of culturally relevant pedagogy. *American Educational Research Journal, 32*(3), 465–491.

Ladson-Billings, G. (1997). It doesn't add up: African American students' mathematics achievement. *Journal for Research in Mathematics Education, 28*(6), 697–708.

Laird, T.F.N., and others. (2007). African American and Hispanic student engagement at minority serving and predominantly White institutions. *Journal of College Student Development, 48*(1), 39–56.

Lam, C. P., and others. (2005). A ten year assessment of the pre-engineering program for under-represented, low income and/or first generation college students at the University of Akron. *Journal of STEM Education, 6*(2–3), 14–20.

Lederman, D. (2010). Recalculating Latino STEM success. Retrieved December 16, 2010, from http://www.insidehighered.com/news/2010/01/05/latino.

Lee, O. (1997). Diversity and equity for Asian American students in science education. *Science Education, 81*(1), 107–122.

Lent, R. W., and others. (2005). Social cognitive predictors of academic interests and goals in engineering: Utility for women and students at historically Black universities. *Journal of Counseling Psychology, 52*(1), 84–92.

Leslie, L. L., McClure, G. T., and Oaxaca, R. L. (1998). Women and minorities in science and engineering: A life sequence analysis. *Journal of Higher Education, 69*(3), 239–276.

Lewis, A. E., Chesler, M., and Forman, T. A. (2000). The impact of "colorblind" ideologies on students of color: Intergroup relations at a predominantly White university. *Journal of Negro Education, 69*(1/2), 74–91.

Lewis, B. F. (2003). A critique of literature on the under-representation of African Americans in science: Directions for future research. *Journal of Women and Minorities in Science and Engineering, 9*(3&4), 361–373.

Lipman, P. (1995). "Bringing out the best in them?" The contribution of culturally relevant teachers to educational reform. *Theory into Practice, 34*(3), 202–208.

Lopatto, D. (2004). Survey of undergraduate research experiences (SURE): First findings. *Cell Biology Education, 3*(4), 270–277.

Lord, C. G., and Sàenz, D. S. (1985). Memory deficits and memory surfeits: Differential cognitive consequences of tokenism for tokens and observer. *Journal of Personality and Social Psychology, 49,* 918–926.

Lundy, G. F. (2005). Peer relations and school resistance: Does oppositional culture apply to race or to gender? *Journal of Negro Education, 73*(3), 233–245.

MacDonald, R., and Korinek, L. (1995). Cooperative learning activities in large entry-level geology courses. *Journal of Geological Education 43,* 341–345.

Majors, R., and Billson, J. B. (1992). *Cool pose: The dilemmas of Black manhood in America.* New York: Touchstone.

Malcom, L. E. (2010). Charting the pathways to STEM for Latina/o students: The role of community colleges. In S. R. Harper and C. B. Newman (Eds.), *Students of color in STEM: Engineering a new research agenda.* New Directions for Institutional Research No. 148, 29–40. San Francisco: Jossey-Bass.

Maple, S. A., and Stage, F. K. (1991). Influences on the choice of math/science major by gender and ethnicity. *American Educational Research Journal, 28*(1), 37–60.

Maramba, D. C. (2008a). Immigrant families and the college experience: Perspectives of Filipina Americans. *Journal of College Student Development, 49*(4), 336–350.

Maramba, D. C. (2008b). Understanding campus climate through voices of Filipino/a American college students. *College Student Journal, 42*(4), 1045–1060.

Maramba, D. C., and Velasquez, P. (forthcoming). Influences of the campus experience on the ethnic identity development of students of color. *Education and Urban Society.*

Massey, W. E. (1992). A success story amid decades of disappointment. *Science, 258,* 1177–1179.

Maton, K. I., and Hrabowski, F. A. (2004). Increasing the number of African American PhDs in the sciences and engineering. *American Psychologist, 59*(6), 547–556.

Maton, K. I., Hrabowski, F. A., and Schmitt, C. L. (2000). African American college students excelling in the sciences: College and postcollege outcome in the Meyerhoff Scholars Program. *Journal of Research in Science Teaching, 37*(7), 629–654.

May, G. S., and Chubin, D. E. (2003). A retrospective on undergraduate engineering success for underrepresented minority students. *Journal of Engineering Education, 92*(1), 27–39.

Mayer, D. P., Mullens, J. E., and Moore, M. T. (2000). Monitoring school quality: An indicators report, NCES 2001-030. Washington, DC: National Center for Education Statistics. Retrieved December 16, 2010, from http://www.nces.ed.gov/pubs2001/2001030.pdf.

McNamee, S. J., and Miller, R. K., Jr. (2009). *The meritocracy myth.* Lanham, MD: Rowman & Littlefield.

Meadows, L., and Jarema, S. (2006). An evaluation of the impact of a service-learning project in a required first-year engineering course. Proceedings of the ASEE Annual Conference and Exposition, Chicago, IL.

Millett, C. M. (2003). How undergraduate loan debt affects application and enrollment in graduate or first professional school. *Journal of Higher Education, 74*(4), 386–427.

Monk, D. H. (1994). Subject area preparation of secondary mathematics and science teachers and student achievement. *Economics of Education Review, 13*(2), 125–145.

Moore, J. L. (2000). Counseling African American men back to health. In L. Jones (Ed.). African American brothers of the academy: Up and coming Black scholars earning our way in higher education (pp. 249–261). Sterling, VA: Stylus.

Moore, J. L. (2006). A qualitative investigation of African American males' career trajectory in engineering: Implications for teachers, school counselors, and parents. *Teachers College Record, 108*(2), 246–266.

Moos, R. H. (1986). *The human context: Environmental determinants of behavior.* Malabar, FL: Krieger.

Moreno, S. E., and Muller, C. (1999). The transition through first-year calculus in the university. *American Journal of Education, 108*(1), 30–57.

Murphey, T. (1995). Identity and beliefs in language learning. *Language Teacher, 19*(4), 34–36.

Murphey, T. (1996). Near peer role models. *Teachers Talking to Teachers, 4*(3), 21–22.

Murphey, T., and Arao, H. (2001). Reported belief changes through near peer role modeling. *TESL-EJ, 5*(3). Retrieved October 5, 2010, from http://tesl-ej.org/ej19/a1.html.

Museus, S. D. (2008a). The model minority and the inferior minority myths: Inside stereotypes and their implications for student involvement. *About Campus, 13*(3), 2–8.

Museus, S. D. (2008b). The role of ethnic student organizations in fostering African American and Asian American students' cultural adjustment and membership at predominantly White institutions. *Journal of College Student Development, 49*(6), 568–586.

Museus, S. D. (2009). A critical analysis of the exclusion of Asian Americans from higher education research and discourse. In L. Zhan (Ed.), *Asian American voices: Engaging, empowering, enabling* (pp. 59–76). New York: NLN Press.

Museus, S. D. (2010a). Delineating the ways that targeted support programs facilitate minority students' access to social networks and development of social capital in college. *Enrollment Management Journal: Student Access, Finances, and Success in Higher Education, 4*(3), 10–41.

Museus, S. D. (2010b). Understanding racial differences in the effects of loans on degree attainment: A path analysis. *Journal of College Student Retention: Research, Theory & Practice, 11*(4), 499–527.

Museus, S. D. (forthcoming). Asian American millennials in college: At the intersections of diversification, digitization, and globalization. In F. Bonner and V. Lechuga (Eds.), *Millennial students of color.* Sterling, VA: Stylus.

Museus, S. D., and Chang, M. J. (2009). Rising to the challenge of conducting research on Asian Americans in higher education. In S. D. Museus (Ed.), *Conducting research on Asian Americans in higher education.* New Directions for Institutional Research (No. 142, pp. 95–105). San Francisco: Jossey-Bass.

Museus, S. D., and Harris, F. (2010). The elements of institutional culture and minority college student success. In T. E. Dancy II (Ed.), *Managing diversity: (Re)visioning equity on college campuses* (pp. 25–44). New York: Peter Lang.

Museus, S. D., Jayakumar, U. M., and Robinson, T. (forthcoming). An examination of the effects of racial representation on the persistence of community college students: An examination of conditional and indirect effects. Manuscript accepted for publication in *Journal of College Student Retention: Theory, Research, and Practice.*

Museus, S. D., and Kiang, P. N. (2009). The model minority myth and how it contributes to the invisible minority reality in higher education research. In S. D. Museus (Ed.), *Conducting research on Asian Americans in higher education.* New Directions for Institutional Research (No. 142, pp. 5–15). San Francisco: Jossey-Bass.

Museus, S. D., and Liverman, D. (2010). Analyzing high-performing institutions: Implications for studying minority students in STEM. In S. R. Harper, C. Newman, and S. Gary (Eds.), *Students of color in STEM: Constructing a new research agenda.* New Directions for Institutional Research (No. 148, 17–27). San Francisco: Jossey-Bass.

Museus, S. D., and Neville, K. M. (forthcoming). Delineating the ways that key institutional agents provide racial minority students with access to social capital in college. *Journal of College Student Development.*

Museus, S. D., Nichols, A. H., and Lambert, A. (2008). Racial differences in the effects of campus racial climate on degree completion: A structural model. *Review of Higher Education, 32*(1), 107–134.

Museus, S. D., and Quaye, S. J. (2009). Toward an intercultural perspective of racial and ethnic minority college student persistence. *Review of Higher Education, 33*(1), 67–94.

Museus, S. D., and Ravello, J. N. (2010). Characteristics of academic advising that contribute to racial and ethnic minority student success at predominantly White institutions. *NACADA Journal, 30*(1), 47–58.

Museus, S. D., and Sevian, H. M. (2009). Factors affecting student trajectories: An examination of the impact of environmental and individual processes on student outcomes in STEM. Unpublished literature review.

Nagda, B. A., and others. (1998). Undergraduate student-faculty research partnerships affect student retention. *Review of Higher Education, 22*(1), 55–72.

National Action Council for Minorities in Engineering. (2008). *Confronting the "new" American dilemma.* Washington, DC: National Action Council for Minorities in Engineering.

National Assessment of Educational Progress (2010). The nation's report card. Retrieved December 18, 2010, from http://nationsreportcard.gov/math_2007/m0009.asp.

National Center for Education Statistics. (2007). *Enrollment in postsecondary institutions, fall 2005; graduation rates, 1999 and 2002 cohorts; and financial statistics, fiscal year 2005.* Washington, DC: National Center for Education Statistics.

National Center for Education Statistics. (2009). *Students who study science, technology, engineering, and mathematics (STEM) in postsecondary education.* Washington, DC: National Center for Education Statistics.

National Center for Education Statistics (2010a). *Fast facts.* Retrieved on December 18, 2010, from http://nces.ed.gov/fastfacts/display.asp?id=171.

National Center for Education Statistics. (2010b). *The condition of education 2010.* Washington, DC: National Center for Education Statistics.

National Consortium on Asian American and Pacific Islander Research in Education [CARE] (2010). *Federal higher education policy priorities and the Asian American and Pacific Islander community.* New York: National Consortium on Asian American and Pacific Islander Research in Education.

National Science Board. (2002). *Science and engineering indicators 2002.* Report No. NSB-02-1. Arlington, VA: National Science Board.

National Science Board. (2004). *Science and engineering indicators 2004.* Washington, DC: National Science Board.

National Science Foundation. (2000a). *Entry and persistence of women and minorities in college science and engineering education.* Washington, DC: National Science Foundation.

National Science Foundation. (2000b). *Women, minorities, and people with disabilities in science and engineering: 2000.* Arlington, VA: National Science Foundation. Retrieved December 16, 2010, from http://www.nsf.gov/statistics/wmpd/pdf/nsf07315.pdf.

National Science Foundation. (2006). *America's pressing challenge: Building a stronger foundation.* Arlington, VA: National Science Foundation.

National Science Foundation. (2010a). *Classification of programs.* Washington, DC: National Science Foundation. Retrieved May 1, 2010, from http://www.nsf.gov/statistics/nsf99330/pdf/sectd.pdf.

National Science Foundation. (2010b). Science and engineering degrees by race/ethnicity. Retrieved December 18, 2010, from http://www.nsf.gov/statistics/nsf10300/content.cfm?pub_id=3786&id=3.

National Science Foundation. (2010c). *Science and engineering indicators 2010.* Arlington, VA: National Science Foundation.

Naylor, J.P.R.D., Pritchard, R. D., and Ilgen, D. R. (1980). *A theory of behavior in organizations.* New York: Agathon.

Nelson-Barber, S., and Estrin, E. (1995). Bringing Native American perspectives to mathematics and science teaching. *Theory into Practice, 34*(3), 174–185.

Ngo, B., and Lee, S. (2007). Complicating the image of model minority success: A review of Southeast Asian American education. *Review of Educational Research, 77*(4), 415–453.

Nora, A., and Cabrera, A. (1996). The role of perceptions of prejudice and discrimination on the adjustment of minority students to college. *Journal of Higher Education, 67,* 119–148.

Oakes, J. (1990). Opportunities, achievement, and choice: Women and minority students in science and mathematics. *Review of Research in Education, 16*(2), 153–166.

Oakes, J. (1995). Two cities' tracking and within school segregation. *Teachers College Record, 96*(4), 681–690.

Oakes, J., Gamoran, A., and Page, R. N. (1992). Curriculum differentiation: Opportunities, outcome, and meanings. In P. W. Jackson (Ed.), *Handbook of research on curriculum* (pp. 570–608). New York: Macmillan.

Padilla, R. V., Trevino, J., Gonzalez, K., and Trevino, J. (1997). Developing local models of minority student success in college. *Journal of College Student Development, 38*(2), 125–135.

Palmer, R. T. (2010a). Counseling diverse students effectively: Building cultural competency among collegiate personnel In T. E. Dancy II (Ed.), *Managing Diversity: (Re)Visioning Equity on College Campuses* (pp. 195–218). New York: Peter Lang.

Palmer, R. T. (2010b). The perceived elimination of affirmative action and the strengthening of historically Black colleges and universities. *Journal of Black Studies, 40,* 762–776.

Palmer, R. T., Davis, R. J., and Maramba, D. C. (forthcoming *a*). The impact of family support for African American males at an historically Black university: Affirming the revision of Tinto's theory. *Journal of College Student Development.*

Palmer, R. T., Davis, R. J., and Maramba, D. C. (forthcoming *b*). Popularizing achievement: The role of an HBCU in supporting academic success for underprepared African American males. *Negro Educational Review.*

Palmer, R. T., Davis, R. J., Moore, J., III, and Hilton, A. A (2010). A nation at risk: Increasing college participation and persistence among African American males to stimulate U.S. global competitiveness. *Journal of African American Males in Education, 1*(2), 105–124.

Palmer, R. T., Davis, R. J., and Thompson, T. (2010). Theory meets practice: HBCU initiatives that promote academic success among African Americans in STEM. *Journal of college student development, 51*(4), 440–443.

Palmer, R. T., and Gasman, M. (2008). 'It takes a village to raise a child': The role of social capital in promoting academic success for Black men at a Black college. *Journal of College Student Development 49*(1), 52–70.

Palmer, R. T., Maramba, D. C., and Holmes, S. L. (forthcoming). Investigating the institutional factors promoting the academic success of students of color. *Journal of College Student Retention.*

Pascarella, E. T., and others (1998). Does work inhibit cognitive development during college? *Educational Evaluation and Policy Analysis, 20*(2), 75–93.

Pascarella, E. T., and Terenzini, P. T. (1991). *How college affects students.* San Francisco: Jossey-Bass.

Pascarella, E. T., and Terenzini, P. T. (2005). *How college affects students: A third decade of research.* San Francisco: Jossey-Bass.

Paulsen, M. B., and St. John, E. P. (1997). The financial nexus between college choice and persistence. *New Directions for Institutional Research, 24*(3), 65–82.

Paulsen, M. B., and St. John, E. P. (2002). Social class and college costs: Examining the financial nexus between college choice and persistence. *Journal of Higher Education, 73*(2), 189–236.

Perna, L., and others. (2009). The contribution of HBCUs to the preparation of African American women for STEM careers: A case study. *Research in Higher Education, 50*(1), 1–23.

Peterson, M. W., and Spencer, M. G. (1990). Understanding academic culture and climate. In W. G. Tierney (Ed.), *Assessing academic climates and cultures.* New Directions for Institutional Research (No. 68). San Francisco: Jossey-Bass.

Powell, L. (1990). Factors associated with the underrepresentation of African Americans in mathematics and science. *Journal of Negro Education, 59*(3), 292–298.

Puma, M. J., and others. (1997). *Prospects: Final report on student outcomes.* Cambridge, MA: Abt Associates.

Pusser, B. (2001). The contemporary politics of access policy: California after proposition 209. In D. E. Heller (Ed.), *The states and public higher education: Affordability, access, and accountability.* Baltimore: Johns Hopkins University Press.

Ramist, L., Lewis, C., and McCamley-Jenkins, L. (1994). *Student group differences in predicting college grades: Sex, language, and ethnic groups.* New York: College Entrance Examination Board.

Rankin, S. R., and Reason, R. D. (2005). Differing perceptions: How students of color and White students perceive campus climate for underrepresented groups. *Journal of College Student Development, 46*(1), 43–61.

Rendón, L. I. (1982). Chicano students in South Texas community colleges: A study of student and institution-related determinants of educational outcomes. Unpublished doctoral dissertation, University of Michigan.

Rendón, L. I., and Hope, R. (1996). An educational system in crisis. In L. Rendon and R. Hope (Eds.), *Educating a new majority* (pp. 1–33). San Francisco: Jossey-Bass.

Rendón, L. I., Jalomo, R. E., and Nora, A. (2000). Theoretical considerations in the study of minority student retention in higher education. In J. Braxton (Ed.), *Reworking the student departure puzzle* (pp. 127–156). Nashville: Vanderbilt University Press.

Rendón, L. I., and Triana, E. (1989). *Making mathematics and science work for Hispanics.* Washington, DC: American Association for the Advancement of Science.

Rochin, R. I., and Mello, S. F. (2007). Latinos in science: Trends and opportunities. *Journal of Hispanic Higher Education, 6*(4), 305–355.

Rolon, A. C. (2003). Educating Latino students. *Educational Leadership, 60*(4), 40–43.

Rosenthal, J. (1993). Theory and practice: Science for undergraduates of limited English proficiency. *Journal of Science Education and Technology, 2*(2), 435–443.

Rowan, B., Chiang, F., and Miller, R. J. (1997). Using research on employees' performance to study the effects of teachers on students' achievement. *Sociology of Education, 70*(4), 669–692.

Russell, M. L., and Atwater, M. M. (2005). Traveling the road to success: A disclosure on persistence throughout the science pipeline with African American students at a predominantly White institution. *Journal of Research in Science Teaching, 42*(6), 691–715.

Sàenz, D. S. (1994). Token status and problem-solving deficits: Detrimental effects of distinctiveness and performance monitoring. *Social Cognition, 12,* 61–74.

St. John, E. P. (1991). A framework for reexamining state resource-management strategies in higher education, *Journal of Higher Education, 62*(3), 263–287.

St. John, E. P. (2002). *The access challenge: Rethinking the causes of the new inequality.* Policy issues report. Bloomington: Education Policy Center, Indiana University.

St. John, E. P. (2003). *Refinancing the college dream: Access, equal opportunity, and justice for taxpayers.* Baltimore: Johns Hopkins University Press.

St. John, E. P., Cabrera, A. F., Nora, A., and Asker, E. H. (2000) Economic influences on persistence reconsidered: How can finance research inform the reconceptualization of persistence models? In J. M. Braxton (Ed.), *Reworking the student departure puzzle* (pp. 29–47). Nashville: Vanderbilt University Press.

St. John, E. P., Paulsen, M. B., and Starkey, J. B. (1996). The nexus between college choice and persistence. *Research in Higher Education, 37*(2), 175–220.

Schmidt, P. (2006). From "minority" to "diversity." *Chronicle of Higher Education, 52*(22), A24.

Schoenberg, R. (1992). Community, culture, and communication: The three Cs of campus leadership. *Liberal Education, 78*(5), 2–15.

Schoenfeld, A. H. (2002). Making mathematics work for all children: Issues of standards, testing, and equity. *Educational Researcher, 31*(1), 13–35.

Sedlacek, W. E. (1987). Black students on white campuses: 20 years of research. *Journal of College Student Personnel, 28*(6), 485–495.

Sedlacek, W. E., Longerbeam, S. L. and Alatorre, H. A. (2003). *In their own voices: What do the data on Latino students mean to them?* (Research Report No. 5-02). College Park, MD: University of Maryland Counseling Center.

Seymour, E., and Hewitt, N. M. (1997). *Talking about leaving: Why undergraduates leave the sciences.* Oxford: Westview Press.

Sheets, R. H. (1995). From remedial to gifted: Effects of culturally centered pedagogy. *Theory into Practice, 34*(4), 186–193.

Shujaa, M. (1995). Cultural self meets cultural other in the African American experience: Teachers' responses to the curriculum content reform. *Theory into Practice, 34*(3), 194–201.

Simpson, J. C. (2001). Segregated by subject: Racial differences in the factors influencing academic major between European Americans, Asian Americans, and African, Hispanic, and Native Americans. *Journal of Higher Education, 72*(1), 63–100.

Smith, D. G., and Wolf-Wendel, L. E. (2005). *The challenge of diversity: Involvement or alienation in the academy?* ASHE Higher Education Report (Vol. 31, No. 1). San Francisco: Jossey-Bass.

Smith, F. M., and Hausfaus, C. O. (1998). Relationship of family support and ethnic minority students' achievement in science and mathematics. *Science Education, 82,* 111–125.

Smyth, F. L., and McArdle, J. J. (2004). Ethnic and gender differences in science graduation at selective colleges with implications for admission policy and college choice. *Research in Higher Education, 45,* 353–381.

Solórzano, D. G. (1995). The doctorate production and baccalaureate origins of African Americans in the sciences and engineering. *Journal of Negro Education, 64*(1), 15–32.

Solórzano, D. G., Ceja, M., and Yosso, T. (2000). Critical race theory, racial microaggressions, and campus racial climate: The experiences of African American college students. *Journal of Negro Education, 69*(1/2), 60–73.

Solórzano, D. G., and Ornelas, A. (2004). A critical race analysis of Latina/o and African American advanced placement enrollment in public high schools. *High School Journal, 87*(3), 15–26.

Sondgeroth, M. S., and Stough, L. M. (1992). *Factors influencing the persistence of ethnic minority students enrolled in a college engineering program.* Paper presented at a meeting of the American Educational Research Association, San Francisco, CA.

Sowell, T. (1993). *Inside American education: The decline, the deception, the dogmas.* New York: Free Press.

Spencer, S. J., Steele, C. M., and Quinn, D. M. (1999). Stereotype threat and women's math performance. *Journal of Experimental Social Psychology, 35,* 4–28.

Steele, C. (1999). A threat in the air: How stereotypes shape intellectual identity and performance. *American Psychologist, 52*(6), 613–629.

Steele, C. M., and Aronson, J. (1995). Stereotype threat and the intellectual test performance of African Americans. *Journal of Personality and Social Psychology, 69,* 797–811.

Strayhorn, T. L. (2010). Undergraduate research participation and STEM graduate degree aspirations among students of color. In S. R. Harper and C. B. Newman (Eds.), *Students of color in STEM: Engineering a new research agenda.* New Directions for Institutional Research (No. 148, 85–93). San Francisco: Jossey-Bass.

Suitts, S. (2003). Fueling education reform: Historically Black colleges are meeting a national science imperative. *Cell Biology Education, 2,* 205–206.

Swail, W. S., Redd, K. E., and Perna, L. W. (2003). *Retaining minority students in higher education: A framework for success.* ASHE-ERIC Higher Education Report No. 2. Washington, DC: School of Education and Human Development, George Washington University.

Takei, I., and Sakamoto, A. (2008). Do college-educated, native-born Asian Americans face a glass ceiling in obtaining managerial authority? *Asian American Policy Review, 17,* 73–85.

Tang, J. (1993). The career attainment of Caucasian and Asian engineers. *Sociological Quarterly, 34*(3), 467–496.

Tate, F. W. (1994). Race, retrenchment, and the reform of school mathematics. *Phi Delta Kappan, 75*(6), 477–484.

Tate, F. W. (1995a). Returning to the root: A cultural relevant approach to mathematics pedagogy. *Theory into Practice, 34*(3), 166–173.

Tate, F. W. (1995b). School mathematics and African American students: Thinking seriously about opportunity to learn standards. *Educational Administration Quarterly, 31*(3), 424–448.

Tate, F. W. (2008). The politics economy of teacher quality in school mathematics: African American males, opportunity, structures, and method. *American Behavioral Scientist, 51*(7), 953–971.

Taylor, E. (2000). Critical race theory and interest convergence in the backlash against affirmative action. *Teachers College Record, 102,* 539–560.

Taylor, E., Gillborn, D., and Ladson-Billings, G. (2009). *Foundations of critical race theory in education.* New York: Routledge.

Teranishi, R. T. (2010). *Asians in the ivory tower: Dilemmas of racial inequality in American higher education.* New York: Teachers College Press.

Thernstrom, S. (1995). The Black-White student mismatch problem in university admissions. *Journal of Blacks in Higher Education, 6,* 62–65.

Thompson, G. L., Warren, S., and Carter, L. (2004). It's not my fault: Predicting high school teachers who blame parents and students for students' low achievement. *High School Journal, 87*(3), 5–14.

Thompson, L., and Lewis, B. (2005). Shooting for the stars: A case study of the mathematics achievement and career attainment of an African American male high school student. *High School Journal, 88*(4), 6–18.

Tierney, W. G. (1992). An anthropological analysis of student participation in college. *Journal of Higher Education, 63*(6), 603–618.

Tierney, W. G. (1999). Models of minority college-going and retention: Cultural integrity versus cultural suicide. *Journal of Negro Education, 68*(1), 80–91.

Tinto, V. (1975). Dropout from higher education: A theoretical synthesis of recent research. *Review of Educational Research, 45*(1), 89–125.

Tinto, V. (1987). *Leaving college: Rethinking the causes and cures of student attrition.* Chicago: University of Chicago Press.

Tinto, V. (1993). *Leaving college: Rethinking the causes and cures of student attrition* (Vol. 2). Chicago: University of Chicago Press.

Tornatzky, L. E., Macias, D. J., and Solis, C. (2006). *Access and achievement: Building educational and career pathways for Latinos in advanced technology.* Los Angeles: Tomas Rivera Policy Institute.

Torres, V., Howard-Hamilton, M. F., and Cooper, D. L. (2003). Identity development of diverse populations: Implications for teaching and administration in higher education. ASHE-ERIC Higher Education Report (Vol. 29, No. 6). San Francisco: Jossey-Bass.

Treisman, U. (1992). Studying students studying calculus: A look at the lives of minority mathematics students in college. *College Mathematics Journal, 23*(5), 362–372.

Triandis, H. C., McCuster, C., and Hui, C. H. (1990). Multicultural probes of individualism and collectivism. *Journal of Personality and Social Psychology, 59*(5), 1006–1020.

Tsui, L. (2007). Effective strategies to increase diversity in STEM fields: A review of the research literature. *Journal of Negro Education, 76*(4), 555–581.

Tyson, K., Darity, W., and Castellino, D. R. (2005). It's not "a Black thing": Understanding the burden of acting White and other dilemmas of high achievement. *American Sociological Review, 70*, 582–605.

Tyson, W., Lee, R., Borman, K. M., and Hanson, M. A. (2007). Science, technology, engineering, and mathematics (STEM) pathways: High school science and math coursework and postsecondary degree attainment. *Journal of Education for Students Placed at Risk, 12*(3), 243–270.

U.S. Census Bureau. (2004a). *We the people: American Indians and Alaskan Natives in the United States.* Washington, DC: U.S. Government Printing Office.

U.S. Census Bureau. (2004b). *We the people: Asians in the United States.* Washington, DC: U.S. Government Printing Office.

U.S. Census Bureau. (2004c). *We the people: Blacks in the United States.* Washington, DC: U.S. Government Printing Office.

U.S. Census Bureau. (2004d). *We the people: Hispanics in the United States.* Washington, DC: U.S. Government Printing Office.

U.S. Census Bureau. (2004e). *We the people: Pacific Islanders in the United States.* Washington, DC: U.S. Government Printing Office.

U.S. Census Bureau. (2008). *An older and more diverse nation by midcentury.* Retrieved April 15, 2010, from http://www.ccnsus.gov/PressRelease/www/releases/archives/population/012496.html.

U.S. Department of Education. (2000). *Entry and persistence of women and minorities in college science and engineering education.* Washington, DC: U.S. Department of Education.

Van Gennep, A. (1960). *The rites of passage.* Trans. M. B. Vizedom and G. I. Chaffee. Chicago: University of Chicago Press.

Varma, R. (2009). Attracting Native Americans to computing. *Communication of the ACM, 52*(8), 137–140.

Villalpando, O. (2004). Practical considerations of critical race theory and Latina/o critical theory for Latina/o college students. In A. M. Ortiz (Ed.), *Addressing the unique needs of Latina/o American students.* New Directions for Student Services (No. 105, pp. 41–50). San Francisco: Jossey-Bass.

Vining-Brown, S. (1994). *Minority women in science and engineering education.* Final report. Princeton, NJ: Educational Testing Service.

Waller, B. (2006). Math interest and choice intentions of non-traditional African-American college students. *Journal of Vocational Behavior, 68*, 538–547. New York: Simon & Schuster.

Walpole, M. (2007). *Economically and educationally challenged students in higher education: Access to outcomes.* ASHE Higher Education Report (Vol. 33, No. 3). San Francisco: Jossey-Bass.

Walters, N. B. (1997). *Retaining aspiring scholars: Recruitment and retention of students of color in graduate and professional science degree programs.* Paper presented at the 22nd Annual Meeting of the Association for the Study of Higher Education, Albuquerque, NM.

Wei, C. C., and Carroll, C. D. (2004). A decade of undergraduate student aid: 1989–90 to 1999–2000. Washington, DC: National Center for Education Statistics.

Weidman, J. (1989). Undergraduate socialization: A conceptual approach. In J. Smart (Ed.), *Higher education: Handbook of theory and research* (Vol. 5). New York: Agathon.

Weiten, W., Lashley, R. L., and Lloyd, M. A. (1991). *Psychology applied to modern life* (3rd ed.). Florence, KY: Wadsworth.

Wenglinsky, H. (1997). How money matters: Models of the effect of school district spending on academic achievement. *Sociology of Education, 70*(3), 221–237.

White, C. J., and Shelley, C. (1996). Telling stories: Students and administrators talk about retention. In I. H. Johnson and A. J. Ottens (Eds.), *Leveling the playing field: Promoting academic success for students of color.* New Directions for Student Services (No. 74, pp. 15–34). San Francisco: Jossey Bass.

White, J. L., Altschuld, J. W., and Lee, Y. (2008). Evaluating minority retention programs: Problems encountered and lessons learned from the Ohio science and engineering alliance. *Evaluation and Program Planning, 31,* 277–283.

Wilkins, A., and Education Trust. (2006). *Yes we can: Telling truths and dispelling myths about race and education in America.* Washington, DC: Education Trust.

Wilson, R. (2000). Barriers to minority success in college science, mathematics, and engineering programs. In G. Campbell, R. Denes, and C. Morrison (Eds.), *Access denied: Race, ethnicity, and the scientific enterprise* (pp. 193–206). Oxford: Oxford University Press.

Wilson, T. D., and Linville, P. W. (1985). Improving the performance of college freshmen with attributional techniques. *Journal of Personality and Social Psychology, 49,* 287–293.

Xiong, Y. S. (2010). State-mandated language classification: A study of Hmong American students' access to college-preparatory curricula. *AAPI Nexus Journal: Policy, Practice, and Community, 8*(1), 17–42.

Yinger, J. M. (1994). *Ethnicity: Source of strength? Source of conflict?* Albany: State University of New York Press.

Young, M. (1958). The rise of the meritocracy. New Brunswick, NJ: Transaction Publishers.

Name Index

Gasman, M., 61, 71
Gasson, S., 72
Georges, A., 58
Gillborn, D., 25
Glasson, G., 56, 57, 59, 69, 70, 76
Glater, J. D., 55
Glennen, R. E., 74
Gloria, A. M., 67, 71, 72, 76
Goel, J., 11, 17
Goldhaber, D. D., 34
Gonzalez, K., 59, 69
Good, C., 35, 36
Good, J. M., 84
Gotanda, N., 25
Grandy, J., 18, 27, 28, 67, 71, 72, 76
Grant, C. A., 54
Grantham, T. G., 37
Green, A., 56, 57, 59, 69, 70, 76
Green, R., 72
Gregerman, S. R., 83
Guiffrida, D. A., 69, 70, 71, 74
Gutstein, E., 41

H

Hackett, G., 76
Hall, E. R., 28, 43
Hall, W., 35, 39, 42, 60, 62, 67, 71, 72, 75, 90
Hall-Greene, D., 76
Halpin, G. (Gerard), 84
Halpin, G. (Glennelle), 84
Hammond, R., 76
Han, J., 27, 28, 61, 63, 64, 75, 76, 91
Haney, C., 54
Hansen, W. L., 56
Hanson, M. A., 31
Hanson, S. L., 9
Harder, J. A., 35
Harper, S. R., 54, 66, 69, 74
Harris, F., 69, 70
Hathaway, R. S., 83, 84
Hausfaus, C. O., 39
Heller, D. E., 56
Helms, J. E., 6
Hernandez, P., 41, 56, 59, 71, 72, 76
Hewitt, N. M., 27, 42, 44, 57, 70, 72, 73

Hill, C. L., 71
Hill, H. C., 34
Hill, K., 47, 48
Hilton, A. A., 4
Hilton, T. L., 43, 76
Holloway, J., 84
Holmes, S. L., 71
Holt, J. K., 44
Hope, R., 30, 39, 40
Howard, J., 76
Howard-Hamilton, M. F., 6
Hrabowski, F. A., 27, 28, 39, 43, 56, 70, 71, 72, 74, 79
Hsia, J., 43, 76
Huang, G., 76, 93
Hui, C. H., 70
Hune, S., 11, 17
Hurtado, A., 54, 56, 59, 63, 66, 67, 68, 73, 74, 75, 76

I

Ikeda, E. K., 17
Ilgen, D. R., 66
Imani, N., 69, 71
Inouye, D. K., 75
Inzlicht, M., 35, 36

J

Jackson, A. P., 71
Jackson, L. A., 76
Jalomo, R. E., 68, 71
James, K., 56, 59
Jarema, S., 84
Jarosz, J., 73
Jencks, C., 54
Johnson, A. C., 72, 74, 93
Johnson, L. B., 54
Johnson, M. J., 56
Johnson, R. M., 68

K

Kaltenbaugh, L. S., 58
Kane, M. A., 56
Kane, T. J., 63
Kanter, R. M., 36

Subject Index

cultural stereotypes and, 69–70; impact on STEM minority student success, 64–70; individualist and competitive cultural values of, 70; STEM climate and climate of, 65–67; STEM culture and culture of, 67–70. *See also* Institutions

Central American STEM students, 20–21*fig*

Child Trends Databank, 38

Chinese American students, 16*fig*

College Board, 11, 57

College costs, 57

Colorblind meritocracy: affirmative action and, 54–55; description of, 53–54

Committee on Prospering in the Global Economy of the 21st Century, 4–5

Cooperative Institutional Research Program, 44

Critical Race Theory (CRT), 25

Culturally relevant K-12 pedagogy, 40–42

D

Detroit Area Pre-College Engineering Program (DAPCEP), 47–48

Detroit Public School System, 47

Dominican STEM students, 20–21*fig*

E

Economic issues: ability to pay for college, 56–57; employment factors, 59–60; financial aid, 57–58; impact of college cost, 57

Emerging Scholars Program (ESP), 80–81

Employment factors, 59–60

Engineering fields, definition of, 8

Ethnicity, definition of, 7

F

"Factors in K–12 Education That Influence Success Among Racial and Ethnic Minority College Students in the STEM Circuit," 24–25

Faculty: influence on STEM student success by, 71–73; pedagogical approaches used by, 72–73. *See also* K–12 teachers

Fijian American students: educational attainment by percentage, 12; educational levels attained by, 17*fig*

Filipino American students, 16*fig*

Financial aid, 57–58

Fourteenth Amendment, 55

G

General Accounting Office (GAO), 58

Grutter v. Bollinger, 55

Guamanian American students, 17*fig*

H

High school dropouts, 38

higher Education Research Institute, 3

Hispanic STEM students: current condition of, 20–22; STEM degree aspirants who completed STEM degrees, 15*fig*; unique challenges facing, 95. *See also* Mexican Americans; Puerto Rican students

Hispanic students: average eighth-grade math scores of, 13*fig*; average fourth-grade math scores of, 13*fig*; change in SAT math scores, 15*fig*; definition of, 8; gains in 4th- and 8th-grade math scores of, 14*fig*; HSIs (Hispanic-serving institutions) serving, 62–63; K–12 education preparedness of, 28–38; K–12 initiatives contributing to SEM preparedness of, 45–51; percentage of national population, 2; research on K–12 culturally relevant teaching of, 40–42; SAT math score gains by, 19; SAT math scores of, 14*fig*; unique challenges facing, 95

Hispanic-serving institutions (HSIs), 62–63

Historically Black colleges and universities (HBCUs), 61–62, 91

Hmong students: educational attainment by percentage, 12; educational levels attained by, 16*fig*

Hopwood v. Texas, 55

Human Capital Theory, 56

I

Increasing Diversity in Engineering Academics program (University of Akron), 47

Indian students, 16*fig*

Institute for Higher Education Policy, 59, 77–78

Institutional agents: academic advisors, 73–74; faculty, 71–73; influence of peers, 74–75

Institutions: HBCUs (historically Black colleges and universities), 61–62, 91; HSIs (Hispanic-serving institutions), 62–63; MSIs (minority-serving institutions), 60–64; PWIs (predominately white institutions), 39, 62, 63–64; STEM student success at minority-serving, 60–64. *See also* Campus environments

J

Japanese American students: educational attainment by percentage, 12; educational levels attained by, 16*fig*

JBHE Foundation, 54

K

K–12 education: contributors to insufficient academic preparation during, 29–38; examining influence on STEM experience by, 27–28; minority students' success and preparedness in, 28–29; promoting minority STEM students success, 38–44

K–12 education disparities: low teacher expectations, 34–35; oppositional culture, 37; premature departure from high school, 38; school district funding disparities and, 29–30; stereotype threat, 35–36; tracking into remedial courses, 30–31; underrepresentation in AP courses, 32–33; unqualified teachers, 33–34. *See also* Racial disparities

K–12 education initiatives: Detroit Area Pre-College Engineering Program (DAPCEP), 47–48; Say Yes to a Youngster's Future, 48–51; University of Akron's Preengineering Program, 45–47

K–12 education success variables: bilingual education, 39–40; culturally relevant teaching, 40–42; early exposure to STEM careers, 42–43; interest in STEM subjects, 43; parental and support involvement, 39; self-efficacy in STEM, 43–44

K–12 teachers: low expectations by, 34–35; unqualified, 33–34. *See also* Faculty

Korean students, educational levels attained by, 16*fig*

L

Laotian students: educational attainment by percentage, 12; educational levels attained by, 16*fig*

M

Marshallese students: educational attainment by percentage, 12; educational levels attained by, 17*fig*

Mathematics fields, 8. *See also* STEM fields

Mathematics Workshop Program (WMP) [UCB], 78–79

Metropolitan Achievement Test (MAT), 50

Mexican Americans: change in SAT math scores, 15*fig*; SAT math score gains by, 19; SAT math scores of, 14*fig*; as STEM students, 20–21*fig*, 22. *See also* Hispanic STEM students

Meyerhoff Program (UMBC), 79–80

Minority-serving institutions (MSIs): description of, 60; HBCUs (historically Black colleges and universities), 61–62, 91; HSIs (Hispanic-serving institutions), 62–63; STEM student success and impact of, 60–64

Mismatch theory, 63–64

Motivation, 75–77

N

National Action Council for Minorities in Engineering, 4, 12

National Assessment of Educational Progress (NAEP), 30

National Center for Education Statistics, 12, 19, 22, 23, 90

National Consortium on Asian American and Pacific Islander Research in Education [CARE], 11
National Science Board, 9, 60, 61
National Science Foundation (NSF), 8, 27, 28, 33, 93
National Survey of Recent College Graduates, 92
National Urban Coalition's Schools Project, 48
Native American STEM students: current condition of, 23–24; impact of employment required by low-income, 59–60; STEM degree aspirants who completed STEM degrees, 15*fig*. *See also* STEM minority students
Native American students: average eighth-grade math scores of, 13*fig*; average fourth-grade math scores of, 13*fig*; change in SAT math scores, 15*fig*; definition of, 8; percentage of national population, 2; population proportion and STEM degrees of, 16*fig*; SAT math score gains by, 19; SAT math scores of, 14*fig*
Native Hawaiian students, 17*fig*

P

Pakistani students, 16*fig*
Parental support/involvement, 39
Peer relationships, 74–75
Predominately white institutions (PWIs), 39, 62, 63–64
Preengineering Program (University of Akron), 45–47
Proposition 29 (California), 55
Psychological factors, 75–77
Puerto Rican students: change in SAT math scores, 15*fig*; SAT math score gains by, 19; SAT math scores of, 14*fig*; as STEM students, 20–21*fig*. *See also* Hispanic STEM students

R

Race/racism: Critical Race Theory (CRT) on, 25; definition of, 7; impact on STEM minority students, 24–25

Racial disparities: affirmative action addressing, 54–55, 63; black students and educational, 19–20; impact on STEM student success by, 24–25. *See also* K–12 education disparities
Racial and ethnic minority students: definition of, 7; REM STEM model on, 88*fig*–90. *See also* STEM minority students
REM STEM model: illustrated diagram of the, 88*fig*; posits and constructs of the, 88–90
Remedial K–12 courses, 30–31
The Rise of the Meritocracy (Young), 53

S

Samoan students, 17*fig*
SAT: affirmative action prompting greater reliance on, 55; math score by selected racial groups, 14*fig*, 15*fig*, 19
Say Yes to a Youngster's Future, 48–51
Science fields, 8
Self-efficacy: as K–12 education success variables, 43–44; STEM minority student success and, 75–77
Shell Company Foundation, 48
South American STEM students, 20–21*fig*
Southeast Asian American students: educational level attained by, 16*fig*; included in AAPI racial category, 11; K–12 culturally relevant teaching impact on, 42; STEM student percentage among, 11–12. *See also* AAPIs (Asian American and Pacific Islanders)
Spaniard STEM students, 20–21*fig*
STEM circuit: bilingual education facilitating success in, 39–40; campus environments impact on, 64–70; colorblind meritocracy and affirmative action impact on, 53–55; defining success in the, 9; definition of, 8–9; impact of economic influences on, 56–60; impact of institutional agents on, 71–75; K–12 education influence on, 27–52; minority-serving institutions/selective institutions impact

on, 60–64; psychological factors impact on, 75–77; STEM-specific opportunity and support programs and, 77–84

STEM culture: alienation, marginalization, and isolation of, 68–69; comparing campus culture and, 67–70; cultural stereotypes of, 69–70; individualist and competitive values of, 70

STEM education: comparing climates of campus and, 65–67; fostering success of minority students, 1, 4–6; implications for future policy on, 93–96; implications for future practice of, 96–98; implications for future research on, 90–93; important trends in racial demographics and, 2–4; K–12 student self-efficacy in, 43–44; key concepts and definitions related to, 6–9; limitations of the volume in examining, 9–10; racial and ethnic minorities in REM STEM model of, 88*fig*–90

STEM fields: definition and list of, 8; K–12 education exposure to, 42–44. *See also* Mathematics fields

STEM minority student success: bilingual education facilitating, 39–40; campus environments impact on, 64–70; colorblind meritocracy and affirmative action impact on, 53–55; examining methods for fostering, 1, 4–6; impact of economic influences on, 56–60; impact of institutional agents on, 71–75; impact of race and racism on, 24–25; implications for future policy supporting, 93–96; minority-serving institutions/selective institutions impact on, 60–64; psychological factors impact on, 75–77; STEM-specific opportunity and support programs and, 77–84

STEM minority students: comparing graduate rates of white and, 63–64; current condition of, 10–24; implications for future research on, 90–93; K–12 education influence on success of, 27–52; mismatch theory on, 63–64; REM STEM model on,

88*fig*–90; STEM education racial demographic trends and, 2–4. *See also* Racial and ethnic minority students; *specific racial/ethnic group*; STEM white students

STEM white students: comparing graduation rates of minority and, 63–64; STEM degree aspirants who completed STEM degrees, 15*fig*. *See also* White students

STEM-specific programs: Biology Undergraduate Scholars Program (BUSP), 81–82; Emerging Scholars Program (ESP), 80–81; Mathematics Workshop Program (WMP), 78–79; Meyerhoff Program (UMBC), 79–80; STEM student success and, 77–84; Summer Undergraduate Research Program (SURP), 82–83; Undergraduate Research Opportunity Program (UROP), 83–84

Stereotype threat: definition of, 35; K–12 education disparities and, 35–36

Summer Undergraduate Research Program (SURP), 82–83

T

Technology fields, 8

Texas, Hopwood v., 55

Thai students, 16*fig*

Tongan students: educational attainment by percentage, 12; educational levels attained by, 17*fig*

U

Undergraduate Research Opportunity Program (UROP), 83–84

University of Akron: Increasing Diversity in Engineering Academics program of, 47; Preengineering Program of, 45–47

University of California, Berkeley, 78

University of California, Davis, 81

University of California Regents v. Bakke, 55

University of Maryland, Baltimore County, 79–80

University of Michigan, 83
University of Minnesota Twin Cities, 82
University of Texas at Austin, 80
University of Texas Law School, 55
U.S. Census Bureau, 2, 6, 10, 19, 23, 30
U.S. Department of Education, 58, 90

V

Vietnamese students, 16*fig*

W

White institutions (PWIs), 39, 62, 63–64
White students: average eighth-grade math scores of, 13*fig*; average fourth-grade math scores of, 13*fig*; change in SAT math scores, 15*fig*; definition of, 8; gains in 4th- and 8th-grade math scores of, 14*fig*; SAT math score gains by, 19; SAT math scores of, 14*fig*. *See also* STEM white students

About the Authors

Samuel D. Museus, Ph.D., is assistant professor of higher education and an affiliate faculty member of the Asian American Studies Program at the University of Massachusetts Boston, where he teaches doctoral-level courses in qualitative and quantitative research methodology, the impact of college on students, and college students of color. His scholarship is focused on college access and success among underserved student populations. His current research is aimed at understanding the role of institutional environments in minority college students' adjustment, engagement, and persistence. Museus has produced more than fifty journal articles, book chapters, and national conference presentations focused on understanding the institutional factors that shape the experiences and outcomes of racial and ethnic minority students in college.

Robert T. Palmer, Ph.D., is assistant professor of student affairs administration in the Department of Student Affairs Administration at the State University of New York Binghamton. Palmer is an active researcher who examines access, equity, retention, persistence, and the collegiate experience of racial and ethnic minorities, particularly Black men at historically Black colleges and universities. His research has two goals: to help promote the access, retention, and success of racial and ethnic minority students and to advocate for the continued relevancy and significance of HBCUs. Palmer's work has been published in national refereed journals, and he has authored well over fifty peer-reviewed journal articles, book chapters, conference papers, and other academic publications. The American College Personnel Association's Standing Committee for Men recognized his research on Black men and also recognized him as an emerging scholar for 2011.

Ryan J. Davis is a **Ph.D.** student in the Higher Education Program at the University of Maryland, College Park. His research examines factors that influence academic preparation and achievement among underrepresented students. He has authored or co-authored twenty publications in the form of journal articles, book chapters, policy reports, encyclopedia entries, and book reviews.

Dina C. Maramba, Ph.D., is an assistant professor of student affairs administration and affiliate faculty in Asian and Asian American Studies at the State University of New York Binghamton. Her research focuses on equity and diversity issues in the context of higher education. Her interests include how educational institutions and campus climates influence access and success among students of color and first-generation college students. As a student affairs practitioner, she has worked closely with STEM students, facilitating their success in college. Having presented her research nationally and internationally, her work has been published in several higher education journals. She also currently serves on the editorial boards of *Journal of Student Affairs Research and Practice, Journal of College Student Development,* and *Journal of Negro Education.*

About the ASHE Higher Education Report Series

Since 1983, the ASHE (formerly ASHE-ERIC) Higher Education Report Series has been providing researchers, scholars, and practitioners with timely and substantive information on the critical issues facing higher education. Each monograph presents a definitive analysis of a higher education problem or issue, based on a thorough synthesis of significant literature and institutional experiences. Topics range from planning to diversity and multiculturalism, to performance indicators, to curricular innovations. The mission of the Series is to link the best of higher education research and practice to inform decision making and policy. The reports connect conventional wisdom with research and are designed to help busy individuals keep up with the higher education literature. Authors are scholars and practitioners in the academic community. Each report includes an executive summary, review of the pertinent literature, descriptions of effective educational practices, and a summary of key issues to keep in mind to improve educational policies and practice.

The Series is one of the most peer reviewed in higher education. A National Advisory Board made up of ASHE members reviews proposals. A National Review Board of ASHE scholars and practitioners reviews completed manuscripts. Six monographs are published each year and they are approximately 120 pages in length. The reports are widely disseminated through Jossey-Bass and John Wiley & Sons, and they are available online to subscribing institutions through Wiley InterScience (http://www.interscience.wiley.com).

Call for Proposals

The ASHE Higher Education Report Series is actively looking for proposals. We encourage you to contact one of the editors, Dr. Kelly Ward (kaward@wsu.edu) or Dr. Lisa Wolf-Wendel (lwolf@ku.edu), with your ideas.

Recent Titles

ORDER FORM SUBSCRIPTION AND SINGLE ISSUES

DISCOUNTED BACK ISSUES:

Use this form to receive 20% off all back issues of *ASHE Higher Education Report*.
All single issues priced at **$23.20** (normally $29.00)

TITLE	ISSUE NO.	ISBN

Call 888-378-2537 or see mailing instructions below. When calling, mention the promotional code JBNND
to receive your discount. For a complete list of issues, please visit www.josseybass.com/go/aehe

SUBSCRIPTIONS: (1 YEAR, 6 ISSUES)

☐ New Order   ☐ Renewal

U.S.	☐ Individual: $174	☐ Institutional: $265
CANADA/MEXICO	☐ Individual: $174	☐ Institutional: $325
ALL OTHERS	☐ Individual: $210	☐ Institutional: $376

Call 888-378-2537 or see mailing and pricing instructions below.
Online subscriptions are available at www.onlinelibrary.wiley.com

ORDER TOTALS:

Issue / Subscription Amount: $ _____

Shipping Amount: $ _____
(for single issues only – subscription prices include shipping)

Total Amount: $ _____

SHIPPING CHARGES:
First Item $5.00
Each Add'l Item $3.00

(No sales tax for U.S. subscriptions. Canadian residents, add GST for subscription orders. Individual rate subscriptions must
be paid by personal check or credit card. Individual rate subscriptions may not be resold as library copies.)

BILLING & SHIPPING INFORMATION:

☐ **PAYMENT ENCLOSED:** *(U.S. check or money order only. All payments must be in U.S. dollars.)*

☐ **CREDIT CARD:** ☐ VISA ☐ MC ☐ AMEX

Card number _____ Exp. Date _____

Card Holder Name _____ Card Issue # _____

Signature _____ Day Phone _____

☐ **BILL ME:** *(U.S. institutional orders only. Purchase order required.)*

Purchase order # _____
Federal Tax ID 13559302 • GST 89102-8052

Name _____

Address _____

Phone _____ E-mail _____

Copy or detach page and send to: **John Wiley & Sons, PTSC, 5th Floor**
989 Market Street, San Francisco, CA 94103-1741

Order Form can also be faxed to: **888-481-2665**

PROMO JBNND

ENABLE DISCOVERY

Introducing WILEY ONLINE LIBRARY

Wiley Online Library is the next-generation content platform founded on the latest technology and designed with extensive input from the global scholarly community. Wiley Online Library offers seamless integration of must-have content into a new, flexible, and easy-to-use research environment.

Featuring a streamlined interface, the new online service combines intuitive navigation, enhanced discoverability, an expanded range of functionalities, and a wide array of personalization options.

WILEY
ONLINE LIBRARY
wileyonlinelibrary.com

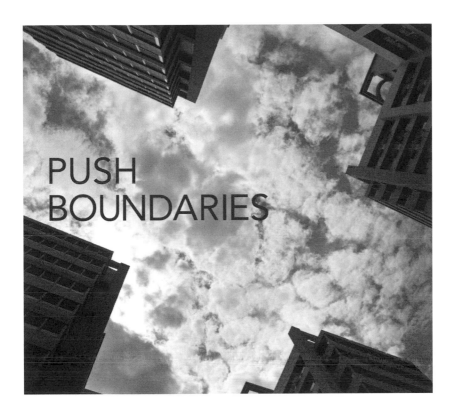

PUSH
BOUNDARIES

WILEY ONLINE LIBRARY
Access this journal and thousands
of other essential resources.

Featuring a clean and easy-to-use interface, this online service delivers
intuitive navigation, enhanced discoverability, expanded functionalities,
and a range of personalization and alerting options.

Sign up for content alerts and RSS feeds, access full-text, learn more
about the journal, find related content, export citations, and click
through to references.